ABLA AMAD was born in Lebanon and arrived
in Australia in 1954 at the age of nineteen.
She has always had a passion for cooking the
food of her homeland and became renowned among
Melbourne's Lebanese community for sharing
wonderful meals in her kitchen at home. In 1979,
at the urging of friends and family, she opened her
restaurant, Abla's, in Elgin Street, Carlton. It has since
become a Melbourne institution and has attracted the
praise of leading food critics and professional chefs.
In 2001 she published her first cookbook, *The Lebanese
Kitchen*, which has been expanded here with the
addition of more than thirty new recipes. In 2011 Abla
was a guest judge on *MasterChef*. She has five children
and lives in North Carlton.

Abla's
Lebanese Kitchen

ABLA AMAD

Photography by Simon Griffiths

LANTERN
an imprint of
PENGUIN BOOKS

*To my beloved husband, John, whose passion
for food stoked the flames of my cooking*

Contents

Introduction

In 2001, the first edition of this book was published; since then, little has changed, except that my willingness to cook and please people has only grown stronger.

Not in my wildest dreams did I imagine that I would put together a cookbook, let alone expect that so many people would enjoy it. Since the publication of *The Lebanese Kitchen* I have been astounded by the countless calls, letters and cards I have received from people around the country (as far afield as Darwin and Perth) and people I've never met, who want to let me know how much they've been delighted by the book.

Countless others – some of whom have become friends – have called simply to say, 'We are cooking from your book and we are thinking of you'. There was even a taxi driver – I never got to know his name! – who for years would drop people off at my restaurant, and who once told me that he would often say to his passengers, especially those from overseas or interstate, 'If you want to eat the best Lebanese food in Melbourne, go to Abla's'.

It should be as plain as day that I have had enormous support, not only from family, close friends and the Lebanese community in Melbourne, but from the wider Australian community as well. It's gratifying for me to know that my cooking has touched the lives of so many. And that's why I am so happy for the opportunity to update and expand the original book.

Now I must say a word or two about the new recipes included in this edition. I can think of only two or three other Lebanese restaurants that were around when I opened my Carlton restaurant in 1979. Today there are hundreds of Middle Eastern restaurants, cafes and bars dotted all over Melbourne (not to mention elsewhere in Australia), but I have many beautiful customers who have been coming to my place for a long, long time – some of them for twenty or thirty years – and now their children and grandchildren are coming along too.

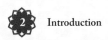

The new recipes are not only personal favourites that I hadn't included in the earlier edition. It dawned on me that there is a new generation who have been exposed to different cuisines and are willing to try them; they are also concerned about what they eat. I have included recipes that tend towards being vegetarian for, on top of liking to eat well, today's young people are health conscious.

Every two years I go back to Lebanon to see what's happening and get some new ideas. I still feel that I'm learning and I've noticed a lot of different influences over the past twenty years – the way of life of the Lebanon I grew up in has changed considerably and so has the cuisine.

But I still love to cook traditional Lebanese recipes, and so let me tell you a story about a dear and loyal customer who has come to my restaurant from the first day it opened. One day he said to me, 'I've sometimes expected something different, but the food hasn't changed'. At first I thought he was going to complain; instead he said, 'Every time I come here the experience is as good as the last, if not better. Abla, I never want you to change'.

It occurred to me while putting together this edition that maybe there are many others like my dear and loyal customer, both young and old, who want to have some lasting link with traditions that are fast disappearing. My best proof of this is my grandchildren, who come to my home for a few hours on a Saturday just so they can learn a couple of recipes from me and not lose touch with their Lebanese heritage. For me, this book is more than a cookbook; I consider it a memoir of my culture as well.

All that is left to say is that I love to cook and, while this may not be the most comprehensive cookbook on Lebanese cuisine, at its heart it has this honest declaration behind it. I hope you feel the same way when you use it and share the pleasure I feel when I sit down to enjoy these dishes with my family and friends.

MENUS

Traditionally, Lebanese people do not sit down to a three-course meal. Whether a large meal is to be served, or just snacks to accompany drinks, it is customary to have a selection of mezza dishes already on the table as your guests arrive. Irrespective of the total number of dishes, there are always olives, *kabbis* (pickles), *labnee* (drained yoghurt), Lebanese bread and a large platter of fresh herbs and vegetables such as cucumber, lettuce, radishes, spring onions, mint and parsley. The vegetables may be eaten on their own or as an accompaniment to the main dishes. The main course at a Lebanese meal consists of a number of dishes, never less than three. If more people arrive, more dishes are prepared. All the main dishes may be put on the table at once, or the hotter dishes may be served later than the cooler ones – it's a matter of preference. The main course always begins with tabbouleh and bread on the table, with the bread being constantly replenished as necessary. A fresh fruit platter is always served at the end of the main meal. The platter consists of seasonal fruits such as oranges, apples, watermelon, rockmelon, stone fruits, cherries and grapes. Coffee is usually served after the fruit. It is often accompanied by a selection of Lebanese sweets. At Easter, semolina-based biscuits called *ma'amoul* (see page 193) are always served.

Meat Menu 1

Mezza: choose 3–4 dishes

Tabbouleh (see page 47)
Tabbouleh

Raw Kibbee (see page 108)
Kibbee nayeh

Baked kibbee with filling (see page 105)
Kibbee bi nayneeyeh

Rolled vine leaves (see page 130)
Ma'hshi warak enib

Purslane salad (see page 148)
Salatat al baqli

Homemade yoghurt (see page 176)
Laban

. . . .

Fresh fruit

. . . .

Lebanese coffee *Ahawe* (see page 212)

. . . .

Selection from, or one of:

Baklava (see page 202)
Baklawa

Sweet cheese with syrup (see page 211)
Halawat el jibeen

Lebanese shortbread (see page 195)
Ghraybi

Semolina slice (see page 199)
Nummoora

Walnut-filled pancakes (see page 206)
Atoyif

Sweet ladies' fingers (see page 201)
Zund el sit

Meat Menu 2

Mezza: choose 3–4 dishes

Mixed Legume Soup (see page 58)
Maklouta

Chicken and rice (see page 84)
Djaj a riz

Lamb on skewers (see page 121)
Lahem Mishwee

Vegetable Stack (see page 164)
Ol'eb Khoudra

Fresh thyme salad (see page 47)
Salatat al Zah'tar

. . . .

Fresh fruit

. . . .

Lebanese coffee *Ahawe* (see page 212)

. . . .

Selection from, or one of:

Baklava (see page 202)
Baklawa

Sweet cheese with syrup (see page 211)
Halawat el jibeen

Sesame biscuits (see page 194)
Barrosi

Date slice (see page 199)
Lafet el balah

Walnut-filled pancakes (see page 206)
Atoyif

Sweet ladies' fingers (see page 201)
Zund el sit

Fish Menu 1

Mezza: choose 3–4 dishes

Monks' soup (see page 60)
Kibet el rahib

Spinach pies (see page 36)
Fatayer bi sabanekh

Fish and rice (see page 69)
Sayyaodien

Bread salad (see page 44)
Fattoush

. . . .

Fresh fruit (including oranges or mandarins)

. . . .

Lebanese coffee *Ahawe* (see page 212)

. . . .

Selection from, or one of:

Baklava (see page 202)
Baklawa

Sweet cheese with syrup (see page 211)
Halawat el jibeen

Sesame biscuits (see page 194)
Barrosi

Doughnuts (see page 201)
Awwamaat

Walnut-filled pancakes (see page 206)
Atoyif

Sweet ladies' fingers (see page 201)
Zund el sit

Fish Menu 2

Mezza: choose 3–4 dishes

Baked fish with tahini and
spicy filling (see page 66)
Samke hara

Fried fish (a selection of red mullet
and garfish) (see pages 70 and 73)
Samke maqli

Pan-fried potato (see page 170)
Bataata maqli

Tahini sauce (see page 19)
Taratour bi tahini

Bread salad (see page 44)
Fattoush

Lebanese garden salad (see page 51)
Salatat al khoudra

. . . .

Fresh fruit (including oranges or mandarins)

. . . .

Lebanese coffee *Ahawe* (see page 212)

. . . .

Selection from, or one of:

Baklava (see page 202)
Baklawa

Sweet cheese with syrup (see page 211)
Halawat el jibeen

Lebanese shortbread (see page 195)
Ghraybi

Date slice (see page 199)
Lafet el balah

Cream caramel (see page 205)
Crème caramel

Sweet ladies' fingers (see page 201)
Zund el sit

Vegetarian Menu 1

Mezza: choose 3–4 dishes (including dips)

Green beans in olive oil (see page 162)
Loubyeh bi zayt

Vegetarian rolled vine leaves (see page 131)
Ma'hshi warak enib

Lentils and rice (see page 155)
Mjadra'at 'addis

Homemade yoghurt (see page 176)
Laban

Purslane salad (see page 148)
Salatat al baqli

. . . .

Fresh fruit

. . . .

Lebanese coffee *Ahawe* (see page 212)

. . . .

Selection from, or one of:

Baklava (see page 202)
Baklawa

Sweet cheese with syrup (see page 211)
Halawat el jibeen

Lebanese shortbread (see page 195)
Ghraybi

Semolina slice (see page 199)
Nummoora

Walnut-filled pancakes (see page 206)
Atoyif

Sweet ladies' fingers (see page 201)
Zund el sit

Vegetarian Menu 2

Mezza: choose 3–4 dishes

Felafel (see page 144)
Felafel

Tahini Sauce (see page 19)
Taratour bi tahini

Silverbeet rolls (see page 146)
Ma'hshi sleeq salak

Pumpkin Kibbee (see page 148)
Kibbee't el jlant

Tabbouleh (see page 47)
Tabbouleh

. . . .

Fresh fruit

. . . .

Lebanese coffee *Ahawe* (see page 212)

. . . .

Selection from, or one of:

Baklava (see page 202)
Baklawa

Sweet cheese with syrup (see page 211)
Halawat el jibeen

Lebanese shortbread (see page 195)
Ghraybi

Sweet dumplings (see page 202)
Mahkroum bi succar

Cream caramel (see page 205)
Crème caramel

Sweet ladies' fingers (see page 201)
Zund el sit

The word 'dip' is a bit of a misnomer in the Lebanese context. In Western cuisine dips tend to have a common meeting point in cocktail or party food, with a wide variety from all corners of the globe being served at the one time, irrespective of their original customs. The 'dips' I offer here, however, are classics in Lebanon and an intrinsic part of the mezza selection. Baba ghannooj, labnee and hummus are classics for good reason. They contain a number of ingredients that are at the foundation of Lebanese cooking – tahini, chickpeas, eggplant, garlic and yoghurt. As you make your way through this book, you will discover that one or more of these ingredients will always be included in a Lebanese repast. And all three dips are, of course, served with another staple: Lebanese bread.

Pickles, or *kabbis*, are a substantial part of Lebanese cuisine. They are served with alcoholic beverages, especially arak, the national drink. Pickles form an integral part of the mezza and are already laid out on the table when guests arrive. In my village in north Lebanon, September and October were a magical time. Coming right after the harvest season, this was the time for drying and pickling an assortment of vegetables to see us through the winter months. The whole village would be abuzz with activity. I have vivid memories of our neighbours gathering in my mother's kitchen to sort through the vegetables and wash and sterilise the glass jars. Then some would pound the olives or slice up the turnips, and the others would boil the eggplants and prepare the filling for pickled eggplants. Like most Lebanese cooks, I do my own pickling for serving at home, as well as the restaurant.

Dips & Pickles

Baba ghannooj

Baba ghannooj

Serves 6–8 as part of a mezza selection

Back in the early days of the restaurant, some of our customers would complain about the smoky flavour of my baba ghannooj – they would insist that it was burnt and send it back to the kitchen. So I would go out and explain that it had to have this smoky flavour, otherwise it wouldn't have been prepared properly. The smoky flavour comes from cooking the eggplants directly over a flame, and it is this flavour that makes the dish. Nowadays baba ghannooj is one of the most popular dishes on our menu and any review of Abla's that mentions it makes a point of its distinctive taste. It's a funny turn of events: in all these years I haven't made a single change to the recipe. It just goes to show how the modern palate has caught up with the taste of an age-old tradition.

Always choose eggplants that are firm and very dark in colour for this classic mezza dish. You can also make it without the tahini; the other ingredients and method remain the same. Without tahini, the dish is called *batinjan m'tabal*.

1 kg eggplants (about 2 large eggplants)
1 clove garlic, roughly chopped
⅔ cup (180 g) tahini
½ cup (125 ml) lemon juice
1 teaspoon salt
1 tablespoon freshly chopped
   flat-leaf parsley
1 tablespoon chopped tomato or
   thinly sliced radish
paprika and extra-virgin olive oil, to serve

Place the whole eggplants directly over a gas flame until blackened and softened, turning regularly to ensure they are cooked evenly. (Alternatively, the eggplants can be pricked with a fork and baked in the oven at 220°C for 40 minutes or until soft and blackened, but this will not produce a smoky flavour.)

Holding on to the stalks, peel the eggplants under cold running water. Chop the flesh and place in a blender with the garlic, tahini, lemon juice and salt. Blend well (this only takes a couple of minutes).

To serve, place the baba ghannooj on a small platter or in a shallow bowl and garnish with chopped parsley and tomato or radish. Sprinkle with paprika and pour over a dash of olive oil.

Yoghurt dip

Labnee

Serves 8–10 as part of a mezza selection

One of the first things I saw when I walked into the kitchen of my new home in Australia was my uncle hanging up a muslin bag filled with yoghurt, with a bowl placed underneath to catch the dripping whey. He was making *labnee*, a kind of cream cheese, which is relished as a dip with other mezza offerings and is also popular at breakfast.

If you like, you can place the finished labnee in a bowl, sprinkle with zah'tar (see page 215) and pour over a little olive oil. Alternatively, mix the labnee with finely chopped tomato, flat-leaf parsley and chopped cucumber before serving.

1 kg natural yoghurt
2 teaspoons salt
extra-virgin olive oil and paprika or zah'tar
(see page 215), to serve

Combine the yoghurt and salt in a mixing bowl, then place in a muslin or cheesecloth bag and tie a knot at the level of the yoghurt. Suspend the bag over a bowl to catch the drips and leave to drain overnight in the refrigerator.

Next day, remove the yoghurt from the bag and place it in a bowl. Drizzle with olive oil and sprinkle with a touch of paprika or zah'tar, then serve.

Garlic paste »

Taratour bi toum

Makes 375 ml

Taratour bi toum is a delicacy enjoyed with chicken and meat dishes, particularly those cooked on the barbecue. Grilled or barbecued lamb, chicken and Kafta on skewers (see page 110) are always accompanied by lashings of toum.

1 medium-sized head of garlic, cloves
**   separated and peeled**
½ teaspoon salt
1 cup (250 ml) olive oil
2½ tablespoons lemon juice

Place the garlic and salt in a food processor and blend to form a fine paste (or use a mortar and pestle), gradually adding the oil, then the lemon juice. If the mixture separates, add another 2 cloves garlic and blend again.

To store, spoon into a 375 ml-capacity sterilised glass jar (see page 215), cover and refrigerate for up to 1 month.

Hummus

Hummous bi tahini

Serves 8–10 as part of a mezza selection

These days, *hummous bi tahini* is familiar to everyone and can be bought ready-made virtually anywhere, but I recommend that you make your own. That way, you can adjust the quantities and make it to the consistency you like, so it will always be pleasing to the palate. Like baba ghannooj (see page 10), hummus is a classic mezza dish.

The chickpeas expand considerably when soaked, so choose a large bowl for soaking. Adding bicarbonate of soda to the soaking water cuts the cooking time by half. If you like, replace the dried chickpeas with three cups of drained tinned chickpeas, and leave out the soaking and simmering, then proceed with the recipe.

1½ cups (300 g) dried chickpeas, washed and
   drained or 3 cups drained tinned chickpeas
1 teaspoon bicarbonate of soda
1½ teaspoons salt
1 clove garlic, roughly chopped
1¼ cups (350 g) tahini
⅔ cup (160 ml) lemon juice
½ teaspoon paprika
flat-leaf parsley leaves, thinly sliced
   radish (optional), extra-virgin olive oil
   and Lebanese bread (see page 24, or use
   purchased), to serve

If using dried chickpeas, cover them with water, add the bicarbonate of soda and soak overnight. The chickpeas should double in volume. Next day, drain the chickpeas, then place in a large saucepan, cover with fresh water and bring to the boil. Reduce the heat to medium, then cover and simmer for 40 minutes or until the chickpeas are very soft. Drain.

Process the salt and garlic together in a food processor. Add the chickpeas (reserving a few to garnish) and blend until smooth, gradually adding the tahini and lemon juice. Stop the processor every now and then to combine the mixture and scrape down the sides. Add 3–4 tablespoons water if you prefer a thinner consistency.

To serve, place the hummus on a small platter or in one or two shallow bowls. Sprinkle with paprika, arrange the parsley decoratively around the edges and pour over a dash of olive oil. Place a few reserved chickpeas or radish slices (if using) in the cente of the bowls and serve with Lebanese bread.

Pickled green olives »

Zaytoun

Makes enough to fill a 2 litre-capacity jar
Suitable for mezza

I'd be very surprised to discover a Lebanese home
without a jar or two of plump green olives always
on hand. For Lebanese people, olives are irresistible
and inevitably kick off any mezza table.

2 kg green olives
2 lemons, cut into 5 mm-thick slices
4–5 wild fennel or dill sprigs
4 hot long red or green chillies (more if desired)
1½ cups (335 g) salt dissolved in 1.5 litres cold water
2 tablespoons olive oil

Using a mallet or a pestle, gently pound the olives one or
two at a time until they split. (Try to do this with one hit
as you don't want to bruise the olives.)

Place the olives in a sterilised 2 litre-capacity pickling jar
(see page 215), evenly distributed with the lemon, fennel
and chillies. Fill the jar with the salty water. Cover and set
aside for about 7 days, then add the oil. Store in a cool place.

The pickled olives will be ready to eat in 3 weeks.
After opening, store at room temperature or in the
fridge for up to 12 months.

Pickled turnips »

Lifit makbous

Makes enough to fill a 1.5 litre-capacity jar
Suitable for mezza

I remember that, as a young girl in Lebanon, when
we pickled turnips we added yeast and salt instead
of the vinegar I've included in this recipe. Often we
would drink the fermented juice from the turnips.
Lifit makbous is usually eaten as a side dish with
Lentils and rice (see page 155).

1.5 kg turnips, washed and peeled
1 beetroot, washed, peeled and sliced
1½ tablespoons salt
2 cups (500 ml) white vinegar, approximately
1 litre water, approximately

Slice each turnip into three rounds, then cut into wedges.
Mix the turnip and beetroot together and place in a sterilised
1.5 litre-capacity pickling jar (see page 215). Add the salt,
then fill the jar with one-third vinegar and two-thirds water.
(No matter the size of pickling jar, I always use this ratio.)
Gently shake the jar to distribute the salt evenly, then seal
and store in a cool, dark place.

The pickled turnips will be ready to eat in 7 days. After
opening, store at room temperature or in the fridge for
2–3 months.

Pickled eggplants

Batinjan makbous

Makes enough to fill a 1.5 litre-capacity jar
Suitable for mezza

The artful combination of garlic, chilli and walnuts stuffed into small eggplants is a much-praised Lebanese delicacy and makes for a very flavoursome addition to the mezza table.

2.5 kg small Japanese eggplants (8–10 cm long),
   stalks removed and cleaned thoroughly
1 tablespoon salt
2 cups (500 ml) white vinegar, approximately
1 litre water, approximately
¼–½ cup (60–125 ml) olive oil

Filling
2 cloves garlic, roughly chopped
6–8 hot long red or green chillies,
   roughly chopped
200 g walnuts
1 tablespoon salt
1 tablespoon olive oil

Cook the eggplants in a saucepan of boiling water for 15–20 minutes or until softened (the eggplants will turn brown). Remove from the pan and place in a bowl of cold water, then leave for 15 minutes. Drain.

To make the filling, put the garlic, chilli and walnuts into a food processor and blend to a coarse paste. Transfer the paste to a mixing bowl, then add the salt and oil and mix well.

Make a 2 cm-deep lengthways incision along each eggplant halfway between the stalk and the base, then squash in 1 tablespoon of the filling; the eggplant flesh will have softened enough to allow you to do this. Place the filled eggplants in a sterilised 1.5 litre-capacity pickling jar (see page 215). Add the salt, then fill the jar with one-third vinegar and two-thirds water. (No matter the size of the pickling jar, I always use this ratio.) Gently shake the jar to distribute the salt evenly, then seal and store in a cool, dark place.

After 7 days, open the jar and fill to the top with oil. Leave uncovered to settle for a few hours as the liquid sometimes overflows, then seal.

The pickled eggplants will be ready to eat in 10–14 days. After opening, store at room temperature for up to 12 months. Cut into slices before serving.

Pickled vegetables

Khoudra makbous

Makes enough to fill a 1.5 litre-capacity jar
Suitable for mezza

There was a time in Lebanon, long ago, when pickled vegetables would only be served during the winter months as fresh seasonal vegetables were not available. However, now they are a popular fixture at any Lebanese meal throughout the entire year. Pickled vegetables are easy to prepare and are a perfect addition to the mezza table.

250 g cauliflower, cut into thick pieces
250 g carrots, cut into slivers
250 g green beans, trimmed
2 hot long green chillies (more or less as desired)
1½ tablespoons salt
2 cups (500 ml) white vinegar, approximately
1 litre water, approximately

Place the vegetables and chillies in a sterilised 1.5 litre-capacity pickling jar (see page 215). Add the salt, then fill the jar with one-third vinegar and two-thirds water. (No matter the size of pickling jar, I always use this ratio.) There is no need to heat the water and vinegar to dissolve the salt, just gently shake the jar to distribute the salt evenly. Seal and store in a cool, dark place.

The pickled vegetables will be ready to eat in 7 days. After opening, you need not store pickled vegetables in the fridge, but they will stay crisp and will keep for 3–4 months if you do so.

Tahini sauce

Taratour bi tahini

Makes 310 ml

Tahini sauce is served with fish and fried vegetables, especially cauliflower (see page 173). If you omit the parsley and do not add extra water, the tahini sauce will keep in the refrigerator for up to two weeks.

½ cup (140 g) tahini
¼ teaspoon salt
1 clove garlic, crushed (optional)
¼ cup (60 ml) water
¼ cup (60 ml) lemon juice
1 tablespoon chopped flat-leaf parsley

Place the tahini, salt and garlic (if using) in a bowl and slowly add the water, stirring continuously. Gradually pour in the lemon juice and stir until smooth, then mix in the parsley. Add more water if you prefer a thinner consistency. If the mixture appears to curdle slightly, gradually stir in a little extra water or lemon juice, until a velvety smooth consistency is achieved.

To store, spoon into a sterilised 375 ml-capacity glass jar (see page 215), then seal and refrigerate. The tahini sauce will keep for 1 week.

Pickled stuffed capsicums

Máhshi flayfale makbous

Makes 6
Suitable for mezza

What is great about this recipe is that it is just as easy to serve it to thirty-six as six people. The variety of ingredients that go into this pickle makes it a treasured addition to any mezza selection and, because it goes a long way, it is considered truly characteristic of Lebanese hospitality.

6 small capsicums, a mixture of red, green and yellow
2 cups (500 ml) white vinegar, approximately
1 litre water, approximately
2 tablespoons salt
olive oil, for topping up

Filling
150 g tender green beans, cut into 1 cm lengths
200 g white cabbage, thinly sliced
200 g cauliflower, thinly sliced
2 carrots, diced
1 eggplant, roughly chopped
¼ cup (30 g) freshly shelled peas
   (or frozen if not in season)
seeds of 1 pomegranate
3 cloves garlic, finely chopped (optional)
2 tablespoons olive oil
2 tablespoons lemon juice
1 teaspoon salt

Take each capsicum and cut around the edge of the stem to create a top (set the tops aside for later). Carefully scrape out as much of the membrane and seeds as possible.

To make the filling, place all the ingredients in a large bowl and mix until well combined. Spoon or use your hands to put the mixture into each capsicum, lightly pressing down as you go to ensure that each capsicum is filled out to the edges. Leave some room at the opening to secure the tops.

Place the stuffed capsicums in a sterilised 1.5 litre-capacity jar (see page 215). Add the salt, then fill the jar with one-third vinegar and two-thirds water. (No matter the size of pickling jar, I always use this ratio.) Leave about 5 mm at the top, then fill to the top with oil. Seal and store in a cool, dark and dry place.

The pickled capsicums will be ready to eat in 2–3 weeks. After opening, store at room temperature or in the fridge for up to 12 months. Slice or cut into wedges before serving.

Bread is a staple of life the world over. Lebanese bread was traditionally cooked on an open-air wood fire, or in a wood-fired oven. I've known people to say a little prayer just before placing their rounds of dough in the oven. There are two types of Lebanese bread: oven bread (khoubiz el firin), and mountain bread (khoubiz el saage). Oven bread is a smaller loaf that puffs roundly and forms a hollow middle while it bakes. When cool, the bread can be split open to make a pocket that is perfect for filling with all sorts of meat, cheese, vegetables and salad. Or it can be torn into bite-sized pieces to scoop a generous amount of hummus (see page 15), baba ghannooj (see page 10) or whatever dip you desire. When made in the traditional way, mountain bread is worked by hand into large, paper-thin rounds that are then laid directly onto a dome-shaped hotplate fuelled by an open fire (see page 28). It is eaten warm, straight off the hotplate.

Traditional savoury pastries are central to the mezza table. Indeed a mezza selection would be incomplete without one or more of the fragrant and delicious pastries featured in this chapter. Lebanese savoury pastries, unlike, say, a traditional English pie, are dainty, elegant-looking parcels with a fragrant and very tasty filling. A lot of love and care goes into making them and that is why they are highly prized by the Lebanese.

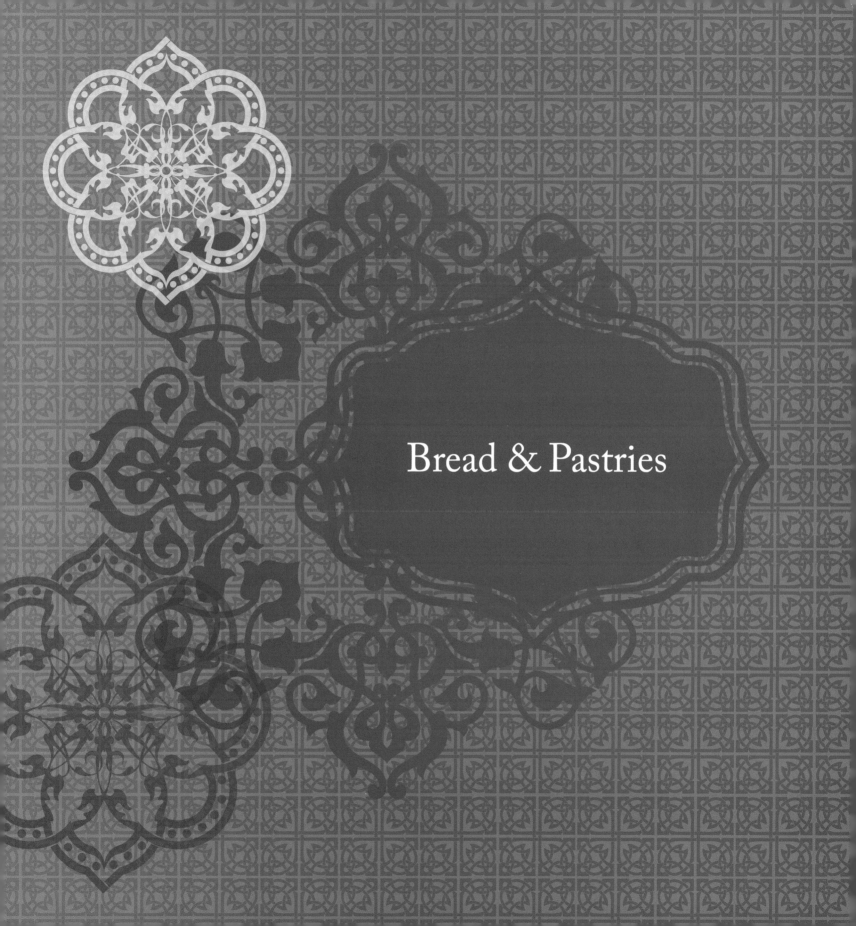

Bread & Pastries

Lebanese bread

Khoubiz el firin

Makes 8

In Melbourne in the 1960s ours was one of the few households to have a wood-fired oven. I have fond memories of friends coming over to assist with making bread. Baking would sometimes be a whole-day event, and the kitchen would be filled with a spirit of community and the aroma of fresh bread. On those days I would find myself trying to keep up with the children's demands for fresh rounds of *khoubiz el firin* spread with lashings of butter and Vegemite!

A word of warning: Lebanese bread will not bake as well in a domestic oven as it will in a commercial or wood-fired one, as it is difficult to get the oven hot enough. However, nowadays there is no need to worry because freshly baked commercially made Lebanese bread is readily available. I've included this recipe for those who really want to have a go at baking Lebanese bread at home. Besides, nothing compares with the smell and taste of bread the moment it comes out of the oven.

3 cups (450 g) plain flour, sifted, plus extra for dusting
1 teaspoon dried yeast mixed with 1 tablespoon water
1¼ cups (310 ml) warm water
½ teaspoon salt

Mix together all the ingredients, then knead until smooth and elastic. Transfer to a greased bowl, then cover with a heavy cloth (even a blanket) and leave to sit in a warm place for 1 hour to rise.

Divide the dough evenly into 8 balls (approximately ½ cup dough each), then cover and leave to rest for another 10 minutes. On a floured surface, flatten out each of the balls with your fingertips until about the size of a saucer (about 9 cm diameter), then roll out to form an 18–20 cm round. Cover and rest again in a warm place for another hour.

Preheat the oven to 240°C and place a baking tray lined with baking paper inside to heat.

Working in batches, place one to two dough rounds on the hot tray and bake for 3–4 minutes until the bread rises. Remove from the oven and leave to cool. Repeat with the remaining dough rounds. Leftover bread can be stored in a freezer bag at room temperature for up to 3 days.

Baked Lebanese bread

Khoubiz muhamma's

Makes 18

These oven-crisped pieces of Lebanese bread resemble corn chips, but their flavour is unmistakeably Lebanese. They are usually served with dips such as Baba ghanooj (see page 10), Hummus (see page 15) and Yoghurt dip (see page 12).

1 round Lebanese bread (see page 24, or purchased)
1 tablespoon zah'tar (optional, see page 215)
1–2 tablespoons olive oil (optional)
1 clove garlic, finely chopped (optional)

Preheat the oven to 180°C.

Split the bread in half horizontally (through the centre) to create 2 rounds and cut each half into quarters, then into bite-sized pieces. Place on a baking tray. Combine the zah'tar and oil, or garlic and oil (if using), then brush over the bread pieces. Bake for 4–5 minutes or until the bread is crisp and golden.

Zah'tar bread »

Mnaeesh bi zah'tar

Makes 6–8

It is now possible to buy zah'tar mixture from Middle Eastern food stores or other specialty food stores and delis, but my mother always dried and mixed her own. I remember she used to lay out thyme sprigs in the summer shade for a few days until they had dried. Then she would pound the thyme in a mortar, adding toasted sesame seeds and sumac, and store the blend in a dry place for when we craved zah'tar bread. Before my mother passed away, she regularly sent her special blend of zah'tar over to me here in Australia.

Tomato and onion is a popular topping for zah'tar bread and the finished rounds resemble mini pizzas. To make, follow the instructions below, then scatter two diced tomatoes and one small diced onion over the zah'tar oil-covered dough, then continue with the recipe. These little breads are known as *Mnaeesh bi zah'tar ou banadoura*.

1 quantity Lebanese bread dough
  (see page 24), risen once
½ cup zah'tar (see page 215)
¾ cup (180 ml) olive oil

Divide the dough into 6–8 pieces and roll out into 4–5 cm rounds. Cover and rest in a warm place for 30 minutes.

Preheat the oven to 240°C. Put the zah'tar into a bowl and gradually stir in enough olive oil to make a moist paste (it shouldn't be runny). Spoon a little over each of the rounds, then place on a baking tray and bake for 10–15 minutes or until cooked. Serve warm or at room temperature.

Kousirra Sukkar's mountain bread

Khoubiz el sorj

Makes 12

My most vivid memory of my mother is of her baking bread on the *sorj* (a dome-shaped metal plate available from Middle Eastern food stores) when I was a young teenager. Every Friday morning she would wake me at dawn, and I'd beg her to take my younger sister to help her make our bread for that week instead of me.

I loved the springiness of the dough that was traditionally left to rise overnight (now I leave it to rise for only an hour and it still works). My mother would place firewood under the sorj and instruct me to roll the dough into large circles the thickness of pancakes. My mother would try to make me forget the pain of rolling so much dough with a story from her youth or tales of one of my father's adventures shepherding goats in the mountains. Without looking, my mother would lift the bread off the sorj and flip it over in a single move. Large spoonfuls of the yoghurt dip, labnee (see page 12) were smeared on the last piece of bread cooked and handed to me to eat in celebration of all our efforts.

This recipe comes from my close friend Koussira, who has worked alongside me at Abla's Restaurant for more than twenty years. Koussira was born and raised in Bsharre, a mountain village in the north of Lebanon. Bsharre is well known as the birthplace and final resting place of the world-renowned writer and artist, Gibran Khalil Gibran.

500 g strong bread flour
500 g wholemeal flour
2 teaspoons dried yeast
2 teaspoons salt
1 litre warm water

Place both flours in a bowl and make a well in the centre. Place the yeast, salt and warm water in the well in the flour and begin mixing. Knead the mixture until it forms a dough – the dough is ready once it stops sticking to your fingers.

Leave the dough in the bowl and cover with a cloth. Place the bowl in a warm area for 1 hour.

When the dough has risen, break it into 12 even-sized balls. Allow the balls to rest for 10 minutes covered with a cloth.

With a rolling pin, roll each ball until it is 2–3 mm thick. It is now ready for cooking on a sorj. Place the rolled dough onto a hot sorj and cook for 3 minutes or until the base is golden. Flip onto the other side and cook for another minute, then serve immediately.

Mountain bread rolls

Serves 1
Suitable for mezza

Mountain bread rolls are easy to make and can be prepared in many different ways and served at anytime of the day. Here are four of my favourite versions of these savoury snacks. They are especially great to take along to your favourite picnic spot and ideal for kids' lunchboxes.

Baba ghanooj and tomato mountain bread roll
1 tablespoon Baba ghanooj (see page 10)
1 round Mountain or Lebanese bread
   (see pages 28 or 24, or purchased)
½ tomato, thinly sliced

Spread the baba ghanooj over one side of the bread and place the tomato on top, evenly spaced, in a line down the centre. Roll up firmly to enclose filling, then cut into 3 cm lengths, transfer to a plate and serve.

Labnee, cucumber and mint mountain bread roll
1 tablespoon Yoghurt dip (see page 12)
1 round Mountain or Lebanese bread
   (see pages 28 or 24, or purchased)
1 Lebanese cucumber, cut into quarters lengthways
3 mint leaves, finely chopped

Spread the yoghurt dip evenly over one side of the bread and place the cucumber on top, evenly spaced, in a line down the centre, then sprinkle with chopped mint. Roll up firmly to enclose the filling, then cut into 3 cm lengths, transfer to a plate and serve.

Kafta mountain bread roll
1 tablespoon Hummus (see page 15)
1 round Mountain or Lebanese bread
   (see pages 28 or 24, or purchased)
1 Kafta skewer (see page 110), meat removed
½ tomato, thinly sliced
1–2 cos or iceberg lettuce leaves, shredded

Spread the hummus evenly over one side of the bread and place the tomato, kafta and lettuce on top, evenly spaced, in a line down the centre. Roll up firmly to enclose filling, then cut into 3 cm lengths, transfer to a plate and serve.

Garlic chicken mountain bread roll
1 tablespoon Hummus (see page 15)
1 round Mountain or Lebanese bread
   (see pages 28 or 24, or purchased)
1 Garlic chicken skewer (see page 82), meat removed
½ tomato, thinly sliced
1–2 cos or iceberg lettuce leaves, shredded

Spread the hummus evenly over one side of the bread and place tomato, garlic chicken and lettuce on top, evenly spaced, in a line down the centre. Roll up firmly to enclose the filling, then cut into 3 cm lengths, transfer to a plate and serve.

Meat and pine nut pastries

Sambousik

Makes 35–40
Suitable for mezza

These fragrant little pastries are only ever served as part of a mezza selection and are considered one of its trophies. While they are best served hot, they may also be eaten cold.

2 tablespoons olive oil, plus extra for deep-frying
¼ cup (40 g) pine nuts
250 g coarsely minced lean lamb
1 onion, chopped
½ teaspoon salt
¼ teaspoon freshly ground black pepper
¼ teaspoon ground cumin
¼ teaspoon ground allspice
½ teaspoon ground sumac (see page 215)

Sambousik pastry
1 cup (150 g) self-raising flour
1 cup (150 g) plain flour, plus extra for dusting
½ teaspoon salt
1 teaspoon sugar
¼ cup (60 ml) olive oil
⅔ cup (160 ml) water

Heat the oil in a frying pan over medium heat and cook the pine nuts for 2–3 minutes or until golden, stirring constantly to prevent burning. Drain on paper towel.

Place the meat in a saucepan and heat gently over low heat. Cook the lamb in its own juices, stirring constantly, for 12 minutes or until the juices have evaporated. Add the onion, salt, pepper and spices and cook for 5 minutes or until the onion becomes translucent. Add the pine nuts, then remove the pan from the heat and set aside.

To make the pastry, sift the flours into a bowl and add the salt, sugar and oil. Gradually mix in the water (you may not need it all) until the mixture comes together to form a rough dough. Knead for a few minutes until smooth and elastic, then return to the bowl. Cover the bowl with a clean tea towel and leave the dough to rest for 15–30 minutes. Divide the dough in half and roll out one piece at a time on a lightly floured surface until about 3 mm thick. Cut out 35–40 rounds using a 6–7 cm cutter.

Place a teaspoon of filling in the centre of each dough round. Bring up the sides to make a semicircle and seal. Press the edges together with the tines of a fork.

Working in batches so as not to crowd the pan, deep-fry the pastries in olive oil over medium heat for 2–3 minutes or until golden and crisp. Drain on paper towel. Serve hot or at room temperature.

Ladies' fingers

Soubih el sit

Makes about 20
Suitable for mezza

Ladies' fingers weren't as popular in Lebanon in the past because you simply couldn't buy filo pastry the way you can now. While you could make it yourself, it takes a lot of time to get the pastry thin enough. These days, because of the widespread availability of filo pastry in Australia, I make ladies' fingers more often than my mother or I ever did in Lebanon.

The ladies' fingers may also be fried in hot oil over medium heat until golden on all sides. This will only take a few minutes.

olive oil, for greasing
1 × 375 g packet filo pastry
1 quantity Meat and pine nut pastries
    filling (see opposite)

Preheat the oven to 200°C and grease a baking tray.

Remove the filo pastry from its packaging but do not unroll. Measure and cut two 8 cm lengths from the roll (return the remaining pastry to its packaging and store in the refrigerator for another use). Cut each of these lengths in half along the fold in the pastry roll.

Unroll a cut portion of pastry, then take 3 strips and place them on top of each other vertically, then place another 3 strips on top of each other horizontally at the base of the pastry strip to form an upside-down 'T'. Place 1 tablespoon of the filling in the centre of the horizontal strip, where the 'T' joins. Bring in the sides and fold over to enclose the filling, then roll along the vertical pastry strip to form a neat cylindrical parcel. Repeat this process until all pastry and filling are used.

Place the ladies' fingers on the baking tray and bake for 15–20 minutes or until golden. Serve hot.

Open meat and tomato pies

Spheha

Makes 18–20
Suitable for mezza

Speha are traditional savoury pastries that are excellent for mezza. While they are best served hot, they are surprisingly delicious when served at room temperature.

The juice of half a lemon may be used instead of pomegranate molasses. However, do not add the juice at the same time as the spices and salt – add it along with the meat and tomato instead.

2 tablespoons olive oil, plus extra for greasing
⅓ cup (50 g) pine nuts
1 onion, finely chopped
½ teaspoon ground allspice
½ teaspoon freshly ground black pepper
1 teaspoon ground sumac (see page 215)
1 teaspoon salt, or to taste
1 teaspoon pomegranate molasses (see page 215)
250 g coarsely minced lean lamb
1 large tomato, finely chopped
1 quantity Sambousik pastry (see page 32)

Preheat the oven to 180°C and lightly grease a baking tray.

Heat the oil in a frying pan over medium heat and cook the pine nuts for 2–3 minutes or until golden brown, stirring constantly to prevent burning. Remove the pine nuts with a slotted spoon and drain on paper towel, reserving the oil.

Place the onion in a bowl and rub in the spices, salt and pomegranate molasses. Add the meat and tomato, then the pine nuts and the reserved oil.

Roll out the pastry until 3–5 mm thick and cut it into twenty 9 cm rounds. Turn the rounds over (this helps the pastry corners stick together) and place 1 tablespoon of filling in the centre of each. Pinch the rounds together at the four 'corners', bringing up the sides to make walls around the filling but leaving the top open (see opposite). If the corners of the pastry will not stick, dip your fingers in water, then dab onto the pastry to dampen the edges.

Arrange the pies on the baking tray and bake for 20–25 minutes or until golden brown. Serve hot or at room temperature.

Spinach pies

Fatayer bi arisheh

Makes 16–18
Suitable for mezza

A mezza feast can last for many hours, so it is customary to offer a wide variety of food in abundant quantities. Serving an array of dainty, golden, savoury pastries such as these is an essential feature of a mezza selection. These lemony spinach pies are another Lebanese favourite.

If preferred, the pies may be cooked in a frying pan. Heat one cup (250 ml) olive oil over medium heat, add the pies and cook for 3–4 minutes or until golden brown on all sides.

1 teaspoon salt
1 bunch spinach, washed and drained, stalks
   removed and leaves cut into 1 cm pieces
2 onions, finely chopped
½ teaspoon freshly ground black pepper
½ teaspoon ground allspice
1 teaspoon ground sumac (see page 215)
1 cup (170 g) raisins (optional)
2½ tablespoons lemon juice
2 tablespoons olive oil
1 quantity Sambousik pastry (see page 32)

Preheat the oven to 200°C and lightly grease a baking tray.

Rub ½ teaspoon of the salt into the spinach and squeeze firmly. Set aside.

Put the onion into a bowl and rub in the spices and remaining salt. Add the spinach, raisins (if using), lemon juice and oil and mix thoroughly. If the mixture is very moist, drain off some of the liquid to stop the pastry becoming soggy.

Roll out the pastry until 3–5 mm thick and cut into sixteen to eighteen 9–12 cm rounds. Place 1 tablespoon well-drained spinach mixture in the centre of each round. Bring up the surrounding pastry into three 'sides', then pull these together into a pyramid shape and press together firmly.

Place the triangles on the baking tray and bake for 30 minutes or until golden brown. The pies are best eaten immediately, but can be served at room temperature.

Cheese and pine nut pastries

Fatayer bi jiban ou snoobar

Makes 18–20
Suitable for mezza

A great side benefit of making the yoghurt cheese, shankleesh (see page 178), is that you can take some of the cheese mixture (which is called *ariseh*) to make these delicious little pastries. Although these pastries are made specifically when we are making shankleesh, fresh ricotta can be used instead.

2 tablespoons olive oil
⅓ cup (50 g) pine nuts
¼ quantity Yoghurt cheese mixture (see page 178), before it is rolled into balls or 500 g fresh ricotta
1 onion, finely chopped
¼ cup finely chopped flat-leaf parsley
1 quantity Sambousik pastry (see page 32)

Preheat the oven to 250°C and lightly grease a baking tray.

Heat the oil in a frying pan over medium heat and cook the pine nuts for 2–3 minutes until golden brown, stirring constantly to prevent burning. Remove the pine nuts with a slotted spoon and drain on paper towel.

Place the shankleesh mixture in a mixing bowl with the onion, parsley and pine nuts and work together until well combined.

Roll out the pastry until 3 mm thick and cut into eighteen to twenty 7 cm rounds. Place 1 teaspoon of the cheese mixture in the centre of each round. Starting at one end, bring up the edges of the pastry and press together to enclose, but do not seal completely. Each parcel should resemble a cone, open at the one end and pointed at the other.

Arrange the parcels on the baking tray and bake for 20–25 minutes or until golden brown. Serve warm.

MEZZA

Mezza is the jewel of the Lebanese table. It is intrinsic to Lebanese cuisine and is the essence of Lebanese hospitality. Mezza is a Middle Eastern word meaning small dishes served hot or cold and shared at the table. It is generally considered the entrée to any meal and is traditionally served with arak, an aniseed-based alcoholic drink. It can consist of up to forty dishes, sometimes more – a banquet in itself that can last for several hours. Without fail, mezza will appear in every Lebanese home. It is incredibly versatile and might consist of a platter of fresh vegetables and herbs: Lebanese cucumbers, tomatoes, cos lettuce, watercress, purslane, mint and thyme. Pickled eggplants, turnips, mixed vegetables and olives would also be served. Cooked vegetables are another addition to the mezza table – fried eggplant, cauliflower and marrow served with Tahini sauce (see page 19).

Many dishes served as part of the mezza can also be eaten as a main course; the recipes for these dishes are in later chapters and their suitability for serving as mezza is indicated at the top of the recipe. Make them in smaller portions than those given if you wish to include them in the mezza selection.

Mezza Menu

Pickled green olives (see page 16)
Zaytoun

Pickled turnips (see page 16)
Lifit makbous

Pickled vegetables (see page 19)
Khoudra makbous

Yoghurt dip (see page 12)
Labnee

Lebanese bread (see page 24)
Khoubiz el firin

Raw kibbee (see page 108)
Kibbee nayeh

Kibbee balls (see page 102)
Kbakeeb

Lamb on skewers (see page 121)
Lahem mishwee

Kafta on skewers (see page 110)
Kafta mishwee

Garlic chicken on skewers (see page 82)
Djaj mishwee bi toum

Chicken wings in garlic (see page 82)
Jawaneh bi toum

Baba ghannooj (see page 10)
Baba ghannooj

Hummus (see page 15)
Hummus bi tahini

Bread salad (see page 44)
Fattoush

Tabbouleh (see page 47)
Tabbouleh

Potato salad (see page 48)
Salatat al bataata

Sliced fresh vegetables

. . . .

Fresh fruit

A Lebanese repast can last for hours, and because we love fresh vegetables and herbs, salads are present throughout the entire meal. They do not come to the table near the close of a meal, nor are they a side order to the main course. The ingredients should be fresh, crisp and full of flavour to tantalise the palate at each and every moment. My personal favourites are the Bread Salad, *fattoush* (see page 44) and the simple Cucumber and Yoghurt Salad, *khiyar bi laban* (see page 51).

Whenever I make these salads I'm reminded of the days when, as a young girl, I collected silk from our silkworms. Around June and July each year my family would have about half-a-dozen girls from the village come to help with the task. After we had collected the silk, cleaned it and then rolled it up, without fail my mother would bring out fattoush and khiyar bi laban because the ingredients were always in abundance. She would also bring dishes like *m'jadra and loubyeh* (lentils and beans). She would prepare these dishes that same morning and have them brought to the silk farm, about 20 minutes away from home. Salads and vegetarian dishes were easy to transport as they didn't need any reheating and we could eat them cold.

Salads

Bread salad

Fattoush

Serves 6 as part of a mezza selection

If tabbouleh is the king of Lebanese salads then *fattoush* is the queen. It's the sumac – a sublime seasoning – and purslane leaves that give this salad its distinctively vibrant palate. I first made fattoush when I was twelve years old and haven't stopped making it since. I recommend serving it with beans or lentils, Pumpkin kibbee (page 148) and chicken or lamb skewers (pages 82 or 121).

Fattoush must be served as soon as it has been tossed with the dressing otherwise the bread will become soggy. Sometimes, as I'm taking the bread out of the oven, I sprinkle it with a little oil to help keep it crisp. You may like to add freshly chopped lettuce leaves and a little crushed garlic.

1 round Lebanese bread (see page 24, or purchased)
5–6 radishes, washed and halved (or quartered if large), then sliced
3 Lebanese cucumbers, washed, halved lengthways, then sliced
4 tomatoes, chopped (about 2 cups)
10 spring onions, chopped (about ½ cup)
1 cup chopped purslane or watercress
1 cup flat-leaf parsley leaves
1 cup mint leaves
½ teaspoon ground allspice
2 teaspoons ground sumac (see page 215)
1 teaspoon salt
½ teaspoon freshly ground black pepper
100 ml lemon juice
100 ml olive oil

Preheat the oven to 180°C.

Split the bread round in half widthways and bake for 4–5 minutes or until golden brown and crisp. Leave to cool, then break into chunky pieces.

Combine all the vegetables and herbs in a bowl and place the bread pieces on top. Mix together the spices, salt, pepper, lemon juice and oil and pour over the salad, tossing gently to combine. Serve immediately.

« Tabbouleh

Tabbouleh

Serves 6 as part of a mezza selection

Tabbouleh is Lebanon's most famous and popular salad. It can be served as an appetiser with the mezza, as a meal on its own or alongside many meat and chicken dishes, including Baked kibbee (see page 105), Lamb on skewers (see page 121) or Garlic chicken on skewers (see page 82). The key to a great tabbouleh is to include an abundant quantity of parsley in relation to the burghul. Follow this recipe to the letter and you won't go wrong.

¼ cup (40 g) fine burghul (see page 214)
5 cups finely chopped flat-leaf parsley
   (about 2 large bunches), rinsed and drained
5 tomatoes, finely chopped (to make 2 cups)
8 spring onions, finely chopped (to make ⅓ cup)
⅓ cup finely chopped mint
150 ml lemon juice
150 ml olive oil
½ teaspoon ground allspice
½ teaspoon freshly ground black pepper
1½ teaspoons salt
baby cos leaves, lettuce leaves, washed and
   quartered or fresh young vine leaves, washed,
   and chopped tomato, to serve

Wash and drain the burghul. Leave to stand for about 30 minutes.

Combine the burghul, parsley, tomato, spring onion and mint in a bowl. Add the lemon juice, oil, spices and salt and mix thoroughly. Place the lettuce leaves or vine leaves on a separate plate or on the side. Garnish with extra chopped tomato, if desired. To eat, cup some tabbouleh in a leaf and enjoy!

Fresh thyme salad

Salatat al zah'tar

Serves 6 as part of a mezza selection

Thyme is such an essential ingredient in the Lebanese kitchen – I cannot imagine a lunch or dinner without the presence of thyme in one form or another. Lebanese people prize it for its evocative aroma and invigorating flavour. In fact, when I first made this salad a friend told me that the ancient Romans believed that people prone to bouts of sadness should sleep on a pillow of thyme to alleviate their condition. After trying this salad I'm sure that you will be convinced that the ancients knew what they were doing!

This recipe calls for fresh and very tender leaves and, whenever possible, I try to select thyme sprigs with longer, pointier leaves.

5 cups thyme leaves, washed and drained
½ white onion, finely chopped
2 tablespoons olive oil
2 tablespoons lemon juice
½ teaspoon salt

Mix together the thyme and onion in a bowl. Add the remaining ingredients and toss gently to combine. Serve immediately.

Purslane salad

Salatat al baqli

Serves 6 as part of a mezza selection

Growing up in Lebanon, I used to find purslane growing wild, but along with endive, baby marrows and Lebanese cucumbers, it was one of the things I couldn't find when I first arrived in Australia. Now you can buy it fresh – the real stuff in beautiful big bunches – from Middle Eastern markets, or you may have to ask your local greengrocer to order some in for you. It is only available when it is in season, which in Australia is in late spring and throughout the summer months. To make the most of this unique ingredient, look for young, tender leaves. Serve this lovely salad as part of a mezza selection or as an accompaniment to a main meal such as Raw kibbee (see page 108), Stuffed whole lamb (see page 118), Baked kafta (see page 111), Stuffed marrows (see page 135) or Chicken and rice (see page 84).

1 clove garlic
½–1 teaspoon salt
1 teaspoon ground sumac (see page 215)
2½ tablespoons lemon juice, or to taste
2 tablespoons olive oil
1 white onion, halved and very finely sliced
5 cups purslane, washed and torn, keeping
   leaves and stems intact
3 tomatoes, diced
2 Lebanese cucumbers, halved lengthways
   and sliced

Using a mortar and pestle, finely crush the garlic with the salt. Transfer to a salad bowl, then add the sumac, lemon juice and oil and mix in the onion. Add the purslane, tomato and cucumber and toss gently to combine. Serve immediately.

Potato salad »

Salatat al bataata

Serves 6 as part of a mezza selection

Try this if you feel like a change from the creamy potato salad often made in Australia – this one is made without mayonnaise. In my first few years here, I made it all the time for barbecues and picnics. My Australian friends thought it was delicious, with a lovely tanginess and sharp taste. The sharpness comes from the combination of olive oil, spices, lemon juice and flat-leaf parsley.

6 potatoes, cut into 3 cm cubes
1 teaspoon salt
3 spring onions, finely chopped
½ cup finely chopped flat-leaf parsley
½ cup finely chopped mint
¼ cup (60 ml) lemon juice
¼ cup (60 ml) olive oil
½ teaspoon freshly ground black pepper
½ teaspoon ground allspice

Boil the potato in a saucepan of salted water for 15 minutes or until tender. Drain and place in a bowl. Add the remaining ingredients and toss gently to combine. Leave to cool before serving.

This salad will keep covered in the refrigerator for up to 3 days.

« Lebanese garden salad

Salatat al khoudra

Serves 6 as an accompaniment

This salad is ideal when offered as a side dish with any of the kibbee dishes on pages 100–108 or with Garlic chicken on skewers (see page 82) or Lamb on skewers (see page 121).

1 cos lettuce, washed and cut into 5 cm pieces
2 Lebanese cucumbers, cut into 3 mm-thick
   slices on the diagonal
1 small white or red onion, halved and very
   thinly sliced (optional)
3 tomatoes, chopped
2 tablespoons mint leaves

Dressing
1½ tablespoons olive oil
2 tablespoons lemon juice
¼ teaspoon salt, or to taste
1 clove garlic, crushed

Place the lettuce, cucumber, onion (if using), tomato and mint in a bowl and mix well. Combine the dressing ingredients and add to the salad. Toss gently and serve.

Cucumber and yoghurt salad

Khiyar bi laban

Serves 6 as an accompaniment

This easy summer salad takes only ten minutes to prepare and makes a lively accompaniment for Baked kibbee (see page 105). When we first came to Australia, my uncle Joe used to bring home telegraph cucumbers that were always three times the size of the cucumbers we were accustomed to. I would ask him, 'But Uncle, can't you get the small ones?' He would say, 'No, no, no small ones. And it's too bad, because the bigger they are, the more expensive they are!' So as soon as he could, he started to grow Lebanese cucumbers in a little patch of earth between his factory and the adjoining house.

2 cloves garlic, peeled
1 teaspoon salt
4 Lebanese cucumbers, peeled,
   quartered lengthways and sliced
1 tablespoon finely chopped mint
1 heaped teaspoon dried mint
800 g natural yoghurt

Using a mortar and pestle, finely crush the garlic with the salt. Transfer to a salad bowl, then add the cucumber, fresh and dried mint and yoghurt and 2 tablespoons water and mix well. Add more water if you prefer a thinner consistency.

Serve immediately as an accompaniment to meat, chicken and vegetable dishes.

Lentil, cucumber and tomato salad with pomegranate seeds

Salatat 'addis, khiyar ou roumayn

Serves 6 as an accompaniment

I came up with this recipe during a mercilessly hot Australian summer. It is a delicate yet still substantial salad, and the sharpness of the lemon juice and pomegranate seeds combined with the dressing makes it especially refreshing. It is an ideal accompaniment to grilled or barbecued fish, chicken or lamb, and can also be served as a light lunch for two people.

½ cup (100 g) green lentils, washed and drained
1 cup flat-leaf parsley leaves
2 Lebanese cucumbers, roughly peeled and
   thinly sliced
2 ripe tomatoes, chopped
1 red onion, quartered and thinly sliced
1 tablespoon finely chopped mint
juice of ½ lemon or 1 tablespoon pomegranate
   molasses (see page 215)
2 tablespoons extra virgin olive oil
½ teaspoon salt, or to taste
seeds of 1 pomegranate
Yoghurt dip (optional, see page 12), to serve

Bring the lentils to the boil in a saucepan with 1½ cups (375 ml) water. When the water starts to boil, add another ½ cup (125 ml) cold water, then reduce the heat to medium and simmer for 5–10 minutes or until the lentils are slightly tender but still a bit firm; be sure not to overcook them. Drain and set aside to cool to room temperature.

Set aside two or three parsley leaves. Place the rest in a bowl with the cucumber, tomato, onion, mint and lentils. Add the lemon juice or pomegranate molasses, olive oil, salt and pomegranate seeds and toss gently to combine. Transfer to a serving platter or shallow bowl. Finish with a dollop of yoghurt dip in the centre (if using), and serve garnished with the reserved parsley leaves.

Spinach and raisin salad with pine nuts

Salatat sabenekh, zbeeb ou snoobar

Serves 6 as an accompaniment

This great salad is easy to make. It is another salad that is equally good served alongside grilled or barbecued meats or as a light meal-in-one.

1 tablespoon olive oil
½ cup (80 g) pine nuts
300 g baby spinach, washed and drained
juice of ½ lemon or 1 tablespoon pomegranate molasses
1 tablespoon extra virgin olive oil
½ teaspoon salt, or to taste
½ cup (85 g) raisins

Heat the oil in a frying pan and cook the pine nuts over medium heat for 2–3 minutes or until golden brown, stirring constantly to prevent burning. Remove the pine nuts with a slotted spoon and drain on paper towel. Set aside to cool.

Place the spinach in a salad bowl and add the lemon juice or pomegranate molasses and olive oil. Sprinkle with salt, then scatter the raisins and pine nuts over the top. Toss gently to combine and serve.

Green leaf and herb salad »

Salatat akhdar

Serves 6 as an accompaniment

The combination of some key Lebanese ingredients (purslane, mint, thyme, sumac and yoghurt) offers a great twist to the everyday green salad. This version is particularly refreshing – as well as healthy.

2 cups purslane leaves, washed and drained
2 cups watercress leaves, washed and drained
2 cups flat-leaf parsley leaves, washed and drained
2 cups mint leaves, washed and drained
½ cup thyme leaves, washed and drained
¼ red onion, very finely sliced
2 tablespoons extra virgin olive oil
juice of ½ lemon
1 tablespoon ground sumac (see page 215)
½ teaspoon salt, or to taste
Homemade yoghurt (see page 176) or
    natural yoghurt, to serve

Place all the leaves and herbs in a salad bowl with the remaining ingredients (except for the yoghurt). Toss gently to combine. Pour a dollop of yoghurt in the centre of the salad and serve.

It is difficult to know why Lebanese soups are not well known outside Lebanon. Perhaps it has to do with the popular myth that the whole Middle East is a vast desert land where it is too hot to eat soup. Yet winter in Lebanon, particularly in the mountainous regions, is freezing. Hence, we have some old-style soups that stave off the bitter cold.

Some of my childhood favourites were made from the beans, grains, pulses and vegetables we dried during summer and stored for winter. The key factor in making these soups is generosity of time, allowing all the ingredients to release their magical flavours. At home in Lebanon it was not out of the ordinary for my mother to tend a cauldron of soup all day long. This was before the arrival of modern cooking methods in villages – a completely different lifestyle from that enjoyed today. Still, whether you intend to serve the following soups as a first course or a main dish, I recommend you also be patient, for the wait is certainly worthwhile. And be sure to accompany each soup with fresh Lebanese bread (see page 24).

Soups

Lentil soup

Shourabat 'addis

Serves 6–8

In the Lebanese kitchen, lentils are mostly prized for their wholesome qualities, which is why *Shourabat 'addis* has been popular in Lebanon for centuries. Featuring the store-cupboard staples of lentils and rice, it is one of a vast repertoire of classic Lebanese peasant dishes, born of necessity to see people through the harsh winter months.

1½ cups (300 g) brown lentils, washed and drained
½ cup (100 g) long-grain rice, washed and drained
2 teaspoons salt
1 tablespoon olive oil
1 onion, finely chopped

Place the lentils and 1 litre water in a large saucepan and bring to the boil over high heat. Reduce the heat to low and simmer, covered, for 30 minutes or until the lentils are tender. Drain. Pass the lentils through a food mill or press through a fine sieve and return to the pan. Add the rice, salt and 1 litre water and bring to a simmer over low heat.

Heat the oil in a small frying pan over high heat and sauté the onion for 2–3 minutes or until translucent. Immediately add to the soup and continue to simmer, covered, for about 1 hour or until the soup thickens (it should be like minestrone). Serve immediately or store covered in the refrigerator and eat within a few days.

Mixed legume soup »

Maklouta

Serves 6

Maklouta is a classic peasant dish, famous throughout Lebanon. Given the wide variety of pulses and grains that go into making this soup, its down-to-earth heartiness is undeniable.

1 cup (200 g) dried chickpeas, washed and drained
½ cup (100 g) dried kidney beans, washed and drained
½ cup (100 g) dried butter beans, washed and drained
½ cup (100 g) brown lentils, washed and drained
½ cup (100 g) long-grain rice, washed and drained (optional)
½ cup (80 g) coarse burghul (see page 214), washed
    and drained
1 large potato, diced
⅓ cup (80 ml) olive oil
1 onion, chopped
1 tablespoon salt
flat-leaf parsley leaves, to serve

Cover the chickpeas, kidney beans and butter beans with water and soak overnight. Next day, drain and transfer to a large saucepan, then cover with fresh water and bring to the boil. Reduce the heat to low and simmer, covered, for 30 minutes. Add the lentils, rice (if using), burghul, potato and enough water to cover.

Heat the oil in a frying pan over medium heat and cook the onion for 5 minutes or until golden brown. Add the onion and oil to the bean mixture, then stir in the salt and ensure the mixture is still covered with water (top up if necessary). Cover and simmer over low heat for about 90 minutes. The soup will be thick – add water if a thinner consistency is preferred. Serve immediately, scattered with flat-leaf parsley or store covered in the refrigerator and eat within a few days.

Silverbeet and lentil soup with lemon

Shourabet 'addis bi haamoud

Serves 6–8

The distinctive tangy flavour of this comforting soup comes from the addition of lemon juice or pomegranate molasses.

⅓ cup (80 ml) olive oil
1 onion, finely chopped
1½ cups (300 g) green lentils, washed and drained
1 tablespoon salt, or to taste
1 small bunch silverbeet (about 600 g),
   well washed and drained
⅓ cup (80 ml) lemon juice or 1 tablespoon
   pomegranate molasses (see page 215)

Heat the oil in a very large heavy-based saucepan or stockpot over high heat and cook the onion for 3–4 minutes until golden brown. Add the lentils, salt and 5 litres water. Stir, cover and bring to the boil over high heat (this will take about 10 minutes).

Trim the ends of the silverbeet stalks and discard, then finely chop the remaining stalks, about 5 mm thick, up to where the stalks narrow to a point, and include some of the leaf. Reserve the remaining leaves for another use, such as making Silverbeet rolls (see page 146).

When the water begins to boil, add another 2 cups (500 ml) cold water (this prevents the lentils from splitting). Cover and bring to the boil again. Add the silverbeet stalks and lemon juice or pomegranate molasses. Reduce the heat to low, then cover and simmer for 30 minutes or until the lentils are tender, stirring occasionally. Taste and add more salt if necessary before serving.

Monks' soup »

Kibet el rahib

Serves 6

The Lebanese have an elaborate tradition of telling stories across the table. These stories quite often involve religious representations of food, and one of my favourites lends colour to the history of this soup. Tradition holds that this was the dish eaten by Mary on the day that Jesus was crucified. To this day *kibet el rahib*, which contains no dairy or meat products, is eaten by Lebanese Christians all over the world on Good Friday.

There are a number of different ways to make this soup. To make a variation known as *'addis bi hammoud* (see opposite), leave out the dumplings and instead add one small bunch of thinly sliced silverbeet leaves (stalks removed).

To make the variation known as *rishta,* follow the recipe opposite, but do not include the lemon juice and replace the dumplings with linguine. If you wish, you can make your own pasta by making the dough recipe for Lebanese 'gnocchi' (see page 156), but use only a quarter of the amount of the ingredients given there. Roll out the dough until very thin and cut into long strips (or use a pasta machine, if you have one). Add the pasta to the boiling soup and simmer until cooked.

1½ cups (300 g) brown lentils, washed and drained
3 cloves garlic, crushed
½ cup (125 ml) lemon juice or 2 tablespoons
   pomegranate molasses (see page 215)
2 teaspoons salt
1 tablespoon olive oil
Lebanese bread (see page 24, or purchased), to serve

Dumplings
½ cup (80 g) fine burghul (see page 214),
   washed and drained
1 small onion, finely chopped
2 teaspoons finely chopped mint
1 tablespoon finely chopped flat-leaf parsley
¼ teaspoon freshly ground black pepper
¼ teaspoon ground allspice
½ cup (75 g) plain flour, sifted
1 teaspoon salt

To make the dumplings, mix together all the ingredients.
Gradually add ¼ cup (60 ml) water until you achieve a dough-
like consistency. Form ½ teaspoon dough into a little round
dumpling. Repeat with the remaining mixture and set aside.

Place the lentils in a large saucepan, cover with water and
bring to the boil. When the water starts to boil, add 1 cup
(250 ml) cold water (this prevents the lentils from splitting),
then cover and simmer over low heat for 15 minutes.

Carefully add the dumplings, then stir in the garlic, lemon
juice or pomegranate molasses, salt and oil. Cover and cook
over medium heat for a further 30 minutes.

Serve immediately with Lebanese bread to the side or store
covered in the refrigerator and eat within a few days.

Red lentil soup

Shourabat 'addis ah'mar

Serves 6

You must have guessed by now that lentils, in one form or another, are a common ingredient in most Lebanese soups. This soup is as simple (and as colourful) as the brown lentil soup, shourabat 'addis (see page 58), and just as tasty.

2 cups (400 g) red lentils, washed and drained
¼ cup (50 g) long-grain rice, washed and drained
1 small onion, chopped
1 teaspoon butter
1 teaspoon salt

Place the lentils in a large saucepan with 1.5 litres water and bring to the boil, covered, over high heat. Reduce heat to low, then add rice and simmer, covered, for 10–15 minutes or until the lentils are tender.

Meanwhile, melt the butter in a small frying pan over high heat and sauté the onion for 4–5 minutes or until translucent. Add to the rice and lentils. Stir in the salt and simmer, covered, for a further 10 minutes. Serve immediately or store covered in the refrigerator and eat within a few days.

Chicken soup »

Shourabat djaj

Serves 6–8

This dish makes a great winter tonic when you're feeling a bit down in the dumps.

1 large skinless chicken breast on the bone
1 cinnamon stick or ¼ teaspoon ground cinnamon
2 bay leaves
1 large onion, finely chopped
1 cup finely chopped flat-leaf parsley, including stalks
2 tomatoes, finely chopped
1 teaspoon salt
½ teaspoon freshly ground black pepper
½ teaspoon ground allspice
½ cup crushed egg vermicelli

Place the chicken breast in a saucepan of water and add the cinnamon and bay leaves. Cover and bring to the boil, then reduce the heat to low and simmer for about 30 minutes (the meat should be starting to come away from the bone). Lift out the chicken and set aside to cool slightly.

Add the onion, parsley and tomato to the pan. Increase the heat to medium and bring to a simmer.

Shred the chicken meat from the bone and cut into bite-sized pieces. Return the chicken to the pan, then add the salt, pepper and allspice and simmer over low heat, covered, for 20 minutes. Add the vermicelli and cook for a further 2–3 minutes. Serve immediately.

The Lebanese are great lovers of fish, and indulge in many ways of cooking it, from the exotic to simple pan-frying (*maqli*). An especially delicious fish recipe is Fish and rice, or *sayyaodien* (see page 69). I think the first time I made sayyaodien was a couple of months after I was married. My brothers, brothers-in-law and their friends came over one Friday night and I made the dish with garfish because that was their favourite. Ever since then, I have made sayyaodien fairly regularly on Fridays.

Fish wasn't hard to get in my youth – we didn't live too far from Tripoli and could get fresh fish directly from the marina there. Alternatively, we'd buy it from local fishmongers. After a catch came in, they would go around the country in their vans, stopping at all the villages to sell their fish. You would select your fish from a bucket and it would be weighed on old-style hand-held scales. Today the fishmongers still visit my village, displaying their wares in crates of ice in the boots of their cars.

Fish

Baked fish with tahini and spicy filling

Samke hara

Serves 4–6

Samke hara is a particular favourite of mine, not only because it originated in Tripoli in North Lebanon, which is not far from where I was born, but because it is a feast for the eyes and genuinely tastes as good as it looks. Any of the pan-fried vegetable dishes (see pages 170–173) would make a lovely accompaniment, as would some of the traditional salads, especially Tabbouleh (see page 47), Bread salad (see page 44) or Purslane salad (see page 48).

While this recipe calls for whole snapper, it can also be made with six 150 g John Dory fillets. Instead of stuffing the fish, you simply spread the filling along one side of a fillet and lay another fillet on top until all the fillets and filling have been used. In this case, you would reduce the cooking time to 10–15 minutes.

2 × 500 g whole snapper, cleaned and scaled
2 tablespoons olive oil
½ teaspoon paprika
flat-leaf parsley leaves, to serve

Filling
4 cloves garlic
1 hot long red or green chilli, chopped
⅓ cup (35 g) walnuts
1 tablespoon chopped coriander
    leaves and stalks
1 tablespoon olive oil
½ teaspoon salt

Tahini sauce
¼ cup (60 ml) lemon juice
¼ cup (70 g) tahini
¼ teaspoon salt

Preheat the oven to 200°C.

To make the filling, use a food processor or mortar and pestle to mince together the garlic, chilli, walnuts and coriander. Add the oil and salt and mix to form a paste.

To make the tahini sauce, combine the lemon juice, tahini and salt well. If you think the sauce is too thick, thin it with a little water.

Make three small incisions across one side of each fish. Fill the incisions and cavity with the filling mixture, then place the fish in a baking dish and pour over the oil. Cover the dish with foil and bake for about 20 minutes. Remove the foil, pour the tahini sauce over and return to the oven for another 5–10 minutes. Sprinkle with paprika, scatter with parsley leaves and serve immediately.

Fish and rice

Sayyaodien

Serves 6

Sayyaodien is another fabled fish recipe to have originated in North Lebanon. Its popularity has since spread along the coast of Lebanon, reaching north into Syria and as far south as Egypt. It takes its name from *sayyad*, the Lebanese word for fisherman, suggesting that it is a dish that they enjoy soon after they return with the day's catch. Although this dish can also be made with fish fillets, I recommend that you use a whole fish as you will need the head and bones to make the quick stock that adds a deliciously strong fish flavour to the dish. Besides, it also a lot easier to judge the freshness of fish bought whole rather than in fillets. If you prefer to use fillets, buy 750 g rockling, monkfish or any other fleshy white fillets. Cut each into four pieces, then heat ⅓ cup (80 ml) oil in a frying pan over high heat and cook the fish for two minutes on each side. Transfer the fish and cooking oil to a saucepan, then add two cups (500 ml) water, cover and cook over medium heat for fifteen minutes. Remove from the heat and strain, reserving the stock and the fish pieces, then continue with the recipe below.

100 ml olive oil
1 × 750 g whole snapper, scaled and cleaned
½ cup (80 g) pine nuts
2 onions, thinly sliced
1½ cups (300 g) long-grain rice, washed and drained
1½ teaspoons salt
¼ teaspoon freshly ground black pepper
¼ teaspoon ground allspice
½ teaspoon ground cumin
¼ teaspoon ground cinnamon

Heat 80 ml of the olive oil in a frying pan over high heat, add the fish and cook for 3–5 minutes on each side. Discard the skin, pull off the flesh and set aside. Boil the fish bones in a saucepan with 2 cups (500 ml) water for about 5 minutes to make stock. Strain, reserving the stock and discarding the bones.

Heat the remaining oil in the same frying pan and cook the pine nuts over medium heat for 2–3 minutes or until golden, stirring constantly to prevent burning. Remove from the pan with a slotted spoon and drain on paper towel. Add the onion to the pan and cook for 5 minutes or until golden. Remove and set aside. Pour another cup of water into the pan and stir until boiling. Transfer to a large saucepan and add the rice, salt, pepper, allspice, fish stock and half of the onion. Stir thoroughly, then cover and simmer over low heat for 20 minutes or until the rice is tender and the stock has been absorbed. If the rice is not completely cooked, add a little more water and cook for a few more minutes until ready.

Spread the rice evenly over a platter. Break the fish into small pieces and spread over the rice. Scatter with the pine nuts and remaining onion. Lightly sprinkle with cumin and cinnamon just before serving. Serve hot or at room temperature.

Fried red mullet

Sultan Ibrahim maqli

Serves 6

The Lebanese love their fish pan-fried, which is referred to by the generic term *samke maqli*. A particular favourite is red mullet, considered the 'king of fish' – hence its name, from a famous sultan of Lebanon.

After you have finished frying the fish, cut one or two rounds of Lebanese bread into quarters and fry in the same oil for two minutes or until golden brown. Serve alongside the fish with pan-fried eggplant or cauliflower (see page 122), potato chips, a freshly made salad such as the Lentil, cucumber and tomato salad with pomegranate seeds on page 52 (see opposite) and Tahini sauce (see page 19).

3 teaspoons salt
1 kg small red mullet (approximately 12 fish),
   cleaned and scaled
½ cup (75 g) plain flour
2 cups (500 ml) light olive oil
2 lemons, sliced or cut into wedges
flat-leaf parsley leaves, to serve

Dissolve 2 teaspoons of the salt in a bowl of water and soak the fish for about 10 minutes. Rinse the fish inside and out under cold running water and pat dry with paper towel. Rub the remaining salt into the fish and set aside for 10 minutes. Roll each fish in flour to coat lightly and evenly (this will prevent the fish from breaking apart as it fries).

Heat the oil to hot in a large frying pan over high heat. Gently lower the fish into the oil – as many as will comfortably fit without overcrowding the pan. Take care as the oil will spatter when you do this. Fry the fish for 3–4 minutes on each side, then remove from the pan and drain on paper towel. Reheat the oil and repeat with the remaining fish.

Arrange the fish on a large platter (or serve the fish straight from the pan) and garnish with the lemon wedges or slices and parsley leaves. Serve immediately.

Fish kibbee

Kibbit samak

Serves 6–8

The word *kibbee* originally meant a combination of burghul and ground meat, but over the years it has come to mean any ingredient that has been ground and mixed with burghul. This particular variation of kibbee came about through observance of the Lenten custom that forbids the consumption of red meat and dairy products. Fish kibbee is a traditional Lebanese Good Friday dish.

2 tablespoons chopped coriander
2 tablespoons chopped mint
1 small onion, roughly chopped
1 teaspoon salt
500–600 g John Dory fillets (or you could use
   barramundi, snapper or rockling fillets),
   cut into cubes
1 cup (160 g) fine burghul (see page 214),
   washed and drained
1 teaspoon ground cumin
½ teaspoon freshly ground black pepper
½ teaspoon ground allspice
½ teaspoon ground cinnamon
¼ cup (60 ml) olive oil

Topping
¼ cup (60 ml) olive oil
¼ cup (40 g) pine nuts
2 onions, finely sliced

Preheat the oven to 220°C.

In a food processor, process the coriander, mint, onion and salt. Add the fish and continue to mince until the mixture is very fine. Place the burghul in a bowl, then add the minced fish, cumin, pepper, allspice and cinnamon and mix well. Process again in the food processor to form a smooth paste (this helps to keep the mixture together when baking).

To make the topping, heat the oil in a small frying pan over medium heat and cook the pine nuts for 2–3 minutes or until golden brown, stirring constantly to prevent burning. Remove from the pan with a slotted spoon and drain on paper towel. Discard some of the oil from the pan. Add the onion and lightly sauté for 5 minutes over low heat or until the onion is translucent, then immediately remove the pan from the heat. Drain the onion on paper towel and mix with the pine nuts.

Place the onion and pine nut mixture in the centre of a lightly greased 26–30 cm round baking dish or tin. Using your hands spread the fish kibbee mixture evenly over the base of the dish. I do this by making small patties of kibbee, placing them close together in the dish over the onion and pine nut mixture, smoothing the surface to push the patties together and form an even layer, with my hands dipped in cold water to prevent the mixture from sticking. Pour the olive oil over the top, then cut into eighths (making 8 wedges), ensuring the incisions are deep. Bake for 30 minutes.

Invert the kibee from the baking dish onto a large platter so the topping is uppermost. Serve hot or at room temperature.

Fried garfish

Samke maqli

Serves 6

It is important to make sure the garfish are thoroughly cleaned. Therefore, although I buy my fish cleaned, I like to place them in a bowl of salty water, remove them one at a time, then scrape off any residual and inside black lining and rinse them under cold water. I then pat them dry with paper towel before proceeding with the recipe.

finely grated rind of 1 lemon
½ cup (75 g) plain flour
1 teaspoon salt
6 whole garfish, cleaned and scaled
1 cup (250 ml) olive oil
lemon wedges, mint sprigs and Silverbeet stalks with
    tahini and lemon juice (optional, see page 161), to serve

Mix the lemon rind with the flour. Salt the fish, then lightly coat them with the flour mixture.

Heat the oil in a shallow non-stick frying pan over high heat, then reduce the heat to medium and cook the fish for 3–4 minutes on each side or until golden and cooked through. Try to only turn the fish once so they remain whole. Serve immediately with lemon wedges, mint sprigs and the silverbeet stalks with tahini and lemon juice to the side (if using).

Pan-fried fish with vegetables

Samke maqli ou khoudra

Serves 6

The Lebanese generally prefer their pan-fried fish to be served with vegetables. To add more verve to the flavour of the fish, I recommend that you cook the vegetables and fish in the same pan. Serve with steamed rice or mashed potato.

1 kg rockling fillets, pin-boned
2 tablespoons plain flour
½ cup (125 ml) olive oil
1 head garlic, cloves separated, peeled and cut
   in half lengthways
3 onions, diced
3 capsicums (green, red and yellow), seeded and diced
6 mushrooms, peeled, stems trimmed and caps diced
3 carrots, diced
1 cup coarsely chopped coriander leaves and stems
1 teaspoon salt
¼ teaspoon ground allspice
¼ teaspoon freshly ground black pepper
½ teaspoon hot paprika
3 tomatoes, diced

Lightly dust the fish in flour. Heat the oil in a large frying pan over medium heat and, working in batches, cook the fish for 5 minutes on each side or until cooked through. Carefully remove the fish from the pan and set aside.

In the same pan, cook the garlic and onion over medium heat for 4–5 minutes or until golden brown. Add the capsicum, mushroom, carrot and coriander and stir. Increase the heat to high, then add the salt and spices and cook for 7 minutes or until the vegetables are soft. Add the tomato, then reduce the heat to low and gently cook for another 5 minutes, stirring regularly. Push all the vegetables to one side, return the fish to the pan and heat through.

Serve the fish with the vegetables spooned over.

When I was growing up my mother, like most of the other villagers, had plenty of chickens running around. She kept them mostly for producing eggs, but she also made sure that at least twelve eggs hatched into chicks every year. A few of these would be fattened up for special occasions. A chicken dish wasn't an everyday affair – it was usually reserved for Sunday lunch or a special barbecue.

Although I love to eat chicken, I think I inherited my mother's extraordinary love of vegetables in preference to poultry or meat. You could tell she loved vegetables because of the funny way she cooked her chicken. It had to be almost burnt. For Sunday lunch, for example, she would marinate the chicken pieces in lemon and garlic, put her own pieces on the grill first and then the rest of the family's. While she served up our share, her pieces were left on the grill until they were almost completely charred. Right up until the day she passed away, she wouldn't eat her chicken until it was well and truly burnt – it truly was a sight to see.

Chicken & Poultry

Chicken livers with garlic

Asbit el djaj bi toum

Serves 6
Suitable for mezza

This quick and easy dish is a great way to serve chicken livers. Make sure you have plenty of fresh Lebanese bread to serve alongside.

1 tablespoon Garlic paste (see page 12) or 4 cloves garlic
2 tablespoons lemon juice
salt
750 g chicken livers
100 ml olive oil
Lebanese bread (see page 24, or purchased), to serve

If you are using garlic paste, whisk it with the lemon juice in a small bowl. If you are using garlic cloves, finely crush them with ½ teaspoon salt, then add the lemon juice and mix.

Cut the chicken livers in half and remove the bile duct and sinew. Heat the oil in a saucepan over medium heat and add the chicken livers. Sprinkle over 1 teaspoon salt, or to taste, then sauté the livers for 5–7 minutes or until browned. Add the garlic and lemon mixture and cook, stirring occasionally, for a further 10–15 minutes or until the centres are cooked.

Serve hot or at room temperature in shallow bowls or on a platter with lots of fresh Lebanese bread.

Chicken casserole »

Yakhanet djaj

Serves 6–8

The trick to cooking this dish perfectly is to cook the chicken just enough so that the meat is soft and succulent but not yet falling apart.

1 tablespoon olive oil
3 large onions, halved and cut into 3 mm-thick semi-circles
1 head garlic, cloves removed and chopped
1 kg skinless chicken breast fillets, cut into 2 cm cubes
1 teaspoon salt
½ teaspoon freshly ground black pepper
½ teaspoon ground allspice
2 heaped tablespoons tomato paste
Lebanese rice (see page 158) and flat-leaf parsley
   leaves, to serve

Heat the oil in a saucepan over high heat and sauté the onion and garlic for 6–7 minutes or until golden brown. Add the chicken, salt, pepper and allspice and stir to combine. Cover and cook for about 15 minutes, stirring regularly. Add the tomato paste, then pour in enough water to cover. Replace the lid and cook for 20–30 minutes, stirring regularly. Scatter with parsley leaves and serve with Lebanese rice.

Baked spatchcocks stuffed with rice and lamb

Farooj ma'hshi

Serves 6
Suitable for mezza

This dish is very similar to Chicken and rice (see page 84). While I make the chicken dish more often, I still get great pleasure when I take six nicely golden spatchcocks from the oven and cut them open to release the aroma of cinnamon from the filling. I like to prepare this when all my children visit or when I've invited a few guests for dinner. It can be cut into smaller pieces and served as part of the mezza table, or as a main course with a little yoghurt and a side dish of Endive in oil (see page 166). The cooking time for spatchcock is not usually this long, however, the extra time is needed to ensure the rice filling is completely cooked. You may want to cover the ends of the legs with foil to prevent them from burning.

6 spatchcocks
1 teaspoon salt
2 tablespoons extra virgin olive oil
mint leaves and purslane sprigs, to serve

Filling
1 cup (200 g) basmati rice
2 tablespoons olive oil
½ cup (70 g) slivered almonds
250 g lean minced lamb
½ teaspoon ground cinnamon
½ teaspoon ground allspice
½ teaspoon freshly ground black pepper
½ teaspoon salt

Preheat the oven to 200°C.

To make the filling, bring 2 cups (500 ml) water to the boil in a saucepan over high heat and add the rice. Parboil the rice for 5 minutes, then drain and set aside to cool.

Meanwhile heat the oil in a frying pan over high heat, reduce the heat to medium and cook the almonds for 3–4 minutes or until golden brown, stirring constantly to prevent the nuts burning. Remove from the pan with a slotted spoon and drain on paper towel.

Cook the lamb in a saucepan in its own juices over medium heat for 10 minutes or until evenly browned and no juices remain, mashing with a wooden spoon to separate any lumps and stirring regularly.

Place the rice, lamb and almonds in a large bowl and sprinkle with cinnamon, allspice, pepper and salt. Mix until well combined.

Take small handfuls of the filling and press gently into the cavity of each spatchcock. Rub the spatchcocks with salt and olive oil, then place them in a large roasting tin. Cover with foil, then bake for 30 minutes. Remove the foil, return the spatchcocks to the oven and bake for another 20–25 minutes or until golden brown.

Serve garnished with mint and purslane sprigs. Carve them into pieces at the table.

Chicken wings in garlic

Jawaneh bi toum

Serves 6
Suitable for mezza

Roast chicken is as popular among the Lebanese as it is with people everywhere. The main difference between Lebanese and Western methods is that the Lebanese usually roast their chicken in pieces rather than whole – this recipe is an example. You can substitute chicken pieces for the chicken wings – the cooking time will be the same. Serve these as part of a mezza selection or as an entrée.

12 chicken wings, wing tips removed and
   cut in half at the joint
1 teaspoon salt
150 ml lemon juice
1½ tablespoons Garlic paste (see page 12) or
   8 cloves garlic pounded with 1 teaspoon salt

Preheat the oven to 210°C.

Wash the chicken wings thoroughly and pat dry with paper towel. Rub the salt over the wings and place in a roasting tin or baking dish. Roast for 20 minutes or until browned.

Mix the lemon juice into the garlic paste or pounded garlic. Remove the chicken from the oven and stir the garlic and lemon mixture through. Return to the oven and roast for a further 20 minutes. Serve immediately.

Garlic chicken on skewers »

Djaj mishwee bi toum

Serves 6–8

This is an ideal dish for barbecues. In days of old this dish would traditionally have been served on a jewelled sword, but as they are hard to come by nowadays I use metal skewers instead. The marinated chicken pieces (minus the skewers) can also be pan-fried over medium heat until cooked through and golden.

If you don't have any Garlic paste (see page 12) on hand to brush over the chicken skewers, quickly pound 4 cloves garlic with ½ teaspoon salt, 2 tablespoons olive oil and 1½ tablespoons lemon juice and use to coat the chicken.

3 large skinless chicken breast or thigh fillets,
   fat removed, cut into 2–3 cm cubes
1 tablespoon Garlic paste (see page 12),
   plus extra to serve
Tabbouleh (optional, see page 47), to serve

Combine the chicken with the garlic paste, then cover and leave to marinate for at least 1 hour.

Thread the chicken onto 6–8 metal skewers and barbecue or grill for 5 minutes or until cooked through and golden brown. Serve hot, accompanied by a bowl of garlic paste and tabbouleh, if desired.

Chicken and rice

Djaj a riz

Serves 6–8

Djaj a riz has become something of a signature dish for me. Generally it is made for special occasions but, as I always insist, every meal is a special occasion! While on a visit to Melbourne more than thirty years ago, an old friend of mine, Barbara, who used to cook for many prominent people in Beirut, showed me the latest trend in presenting the dish in Lebanon. She rummaged through my cupboards for a bowl and instead happened upon a cake tin. In time, I made a slight variation by choosing a tin with a hollow centre, but ever since that day I haven't wavered from creating my chicken and rice dish in a cake tin.

Another way of serving this is to put the lamb and rice mixture on a serving dish and cover it with the chicken. Top with the slivered almonds and pine nuts, and finish with a dusting of ground cinnamon.

2 × 500–600 g whole chicken breasts on the bone, skin on
1 cinnamon stick
2½ teaspoons salt
600 g coarsely minced lean lamb
20 g butter
½ teaspoon freshly ground black pepper
½ teaspoon ground allspice
½ teaspoon ground cinnamon, plus extra to garnish
1½ cups (300 g) long-grain rice, washed and drained
olive oil, for cooking
½ cup (80 g) pine nuts
½ cup (40 g) flaked or slivered almonds

Place the chicken breasts in a large saucepan and cover with water. Add the cinnamon stick and 1 teaspoon of the salt and bring to the boil, then reduce the heat to low and simmer, covered, for 20–30 minutes or until tender and cooked through. Drain, reserving the stock. Remove the skin and tear the meat from the bone (the chicken slivers can be any size). Set aside.

Cook the minced lamb in a saucepan in its own juices over medium heat for about 10 minutes, mashing with a wooden spoon to separate any lumps and stirring regularly to avoid sticking. Stir in the butter, spices and the remaining salt. Cover and cook for 20 minutes or until well done, stirring regularly to prevent lumps forming. Add the rice and 2½ cups (625 ml) of the reserved chicken stock, then cover and cook for a further 20 minutes.

Heat a little olive oil in a frying pan and cook the pine nuts and almonds over medium heat for 3–4 minutes or until golden, stirring constantly to prevent burning. Remove the nuts with a slotted spoon and drain on paper towel.

To assemble, spread the almonds and pine nuts over the base of a round 25 cm cake tin with a hollow centre. Pack the shredded chicken around the outer edge of the mould. Fill with the lamb and rice mixture, pressing down firmly and ensuring the chicken remains in place.

To serve, put a serving plate face down over the mould and invert the chicken and rice onto it. Gently remove the mould and sprinkle a little extra cinnamon over the top.

Baked quail stuffed with spinach, rice, almonds and raisins

Siman ma'hshi

Serves 6
Suitable for mezza

Small and plump quail have long been a part of the mezza tradition because they come out of the oven exquisitely golden and crisp. I recommend that the quail be bought fresh (never frozen!) and cooked on the same day.

6 quail
2 tablespoons lemon juice
2 tablespoons extra virgin olive oil
wilted spinach (optional), to serve

Filling
½ cup (100 g) basmati rice
1½ tablespoons olive oil
½ cup (80 g) pine nuts
¼ cup (40 g) blanched almonds, halved
100 g spinach, washed, drained and coarsely chopped
4 spring onions, finely chopped
½ cup (85 g) raisins
¼ teaspoon ground allspice
¼ teaspoon finely ground black pepper
½ teaspoon salt
1 tablespoon lemon juice

Preheat the oven to 250°C. Lightly grease a large baking dish.

To make the filling, bring 2 cups (500 ml) water to the boil in a saucepan over high heat, then add the rice. Parboil for about 5 minutes, then drain and set aside to cool.

Meanwhile, heat 2 teaspoons of the oil in a frying pan over medium heat and cook the pine nuts and almonds for 2–3 minutes or until golden brown, stirring constantly to prevent burning. Remove the nuts with a slotted spoon and drain on paper towel.

Place the cooled rice, spinach, spring onion, raisins, almonds and pine nuts in a large mixing bowl and sprinkle with the allspice, pepper and salt. Add the lemon juice and remaining olive oil and mix them together until well combined.

Take small handfuls of the filling and gently press into the cavity of each quail. Place the birds on their sides in the baking dish and brush with the combined lemon juice and oil.

Cover with foil and bake for 45 minutes or until golden, basting occasionally with the remaining lemon juice and oil mixture and turning halfway through cooking.

Serve with wilted spinach or as part of a mezza selection.

Ladies' fingers
with chicken

Soubih il sit bi djaj

Makes 20
Suitable for mezza

This is a chicken-based alternative to the more traditional lamb-filled Ladies' Fingers (see page 35) – they are just as delicate and as flavourful as the original version.

For a livelier burst of flavour when you bite into the ladies' fingers, combine 1 tablespoon tahini, the juice of one lemon and ¼ teaspoon salt in a small bowl. Add to the filling mixture below and continue with the recipe.

1 × 375 g packet filo pastry
olive oil, for shallow-frying
Tahini sauce (optional, see page 19), to serve

Filling
¼ cup (60 ml) olive oil
1 large onion, finely chopped
600 g minced chicken breast
½ teaspoon salt
¼ teaspoon ground allspice
¼ teaspoon freshly ground black pepper
¼ teaspoon ground cinnamon
½ cup finely chopped flat-leaf parsley

To make the filling, heat the oil in a frying pan over high heat and sauté the onion for 6–7 minutes or until golden brown. Add the chicken, salt, allspice and pepper, mashing with a wooden spoon to separate any lumps. Add the cinnamon and parsley and cook for 5 minutes or until the chicken mince has browned, stirring regularly. Remove from the heat and cool to room temperature.

Remove the filo pastry from its packaging but do not unroll. Measure and cut two 8 cm lengths from the roll (return the remaining pastry to its packaging and store in the refrigerator for another use). Cut each of these lengths in half along the fold in the pastry roll.

Unroll a cut portion of pastry, then take 3 strips and place them on top of each other vertically, then place another 3 strips on top of each other horizontally at the base of the pastry strip to form an upside-down 'T'. Place 1 tablespoon of the filling in the centre of the horizontal strip, where the 'T' joins. Bring in the sides and fold over to enclose the filling, then roll along the vertical pastry strip to form a neat cylindrical parcel. Repeat this process until all pastry and filling are used.

Heat the oil in a shallow frying pan over low heat. Add the ladies' fingers in batches and cook for about 1 minute or until golden brown all over. Serve hot.

Alternatively, place the ladies' fingers on a baking tray and bake in a 200°C oven for 15–20 minutes or until golden. Serve hot with tahini sauce, if desired.

Chicken breast rolls filled with spinach, rice, pine nuts, almonds and raisins

Safeenat djaj ma'hshi

Serves 6
Suitable for mezza

This dish is similar to the Baked quail on page 89, but it is much easier to make. It can be served as a main meal or as part of a mezza selection. If served as a mezza dish, cut each roll into four or five portions to ensure there is enough to go around. If serving it as a main I suggest offering a vegetable dish such as the Vegetable stack on page 164, Potato salad on page 48 or roasted potato and pumpkin.

6 chicken breast fillets
1 tablespoon olive oil
½ teaspoon salt
¼ teaspoon ground allspice
¼ teaspoon freshly ground black pepper
2 tablespoons lemon juice
2 tablespoons extra virgin olive oil
spinach leaves and Potato salad (optional,
   see page 48), to serve

Filling
½ cup (100 g) basmati rice
1½ tablespoons olive oil
½ cup (80 g) pine nuts
¼ cup (40 g) blanched almonds, halved
100 g spinach, washed, drained and coarsely chopped
4 spring onions, finely chopped (about ½ cup)
½ cup (85 g) raisins
¼ teaspoon ground allspice
¼ teaspoon finely ground black pepper
½ teaspoon salt
1 tablespoon lemon juice

Preheat the oven to 250°C and line a baking tray with baking paper.

To make the filling, bring 2 cups (500 ml) water to the boil in a saucepan over high heat, then add the rice. Parboil for about 5 minutes, then drain and set aside to cool.

Meanwhile, heat 2 teaspoons of the olive oil in a frying pan over medium heat and cook the pine nuts and almonds for 3–4 minutes or until golden brown, stirring constantly to prevent burning. Remove with a slotted spoon and drain on paper towel.

Place the cooled rice, spinach, spring onion, raisins, almonds and pine nuts in a large mixing bowl and sprinkle with the allspice, pepper and salt. Add the lemon juice and remaining oil and mix until well combined.

To butterfly the chicken breasts, cut through the breast widthways from one side to the other but do not cut all the way through. Unfold the breast to form two 'wings', then place a handful of the filling at one end of each chicken breast and roll up. Secure with toothpicks.

Heat the olive oil in a frying pan over medium heat and sear the chicken rolls until evenly golden all over. Transfer to the baking tray, seam-side down, and carefully remove the toothpicks. Season with salt, allspice and pepper and bake for 20–25 minutes, basting occasionally with the combined lemon juice and extra virgin olive oil. Serve immediately with spinach leaves and potato salad to the side.

BARBECUE

I'm not sure what the origins of the barbecue in Australia are, but I believe that in the Middle East the barbecue has its roots in Bedouin culture, where open-air cooking was a necessary part of life. Australians and Lebanese share their love of a good barbecue. However, there are a couple of subtle cultural differences. In Australian culture, a barbecue invitation is usually to an informal outdoor event, and quite often you are expected to not only bring your own drinks, but to bring your own meat too. For the Lebanese, a barbecue invitation can be to an event as informal as a casual get-together similar to offering a cup of coffee, or to a formal sit-down dinner, regardless of whether you are an acquaintance, a close friend, family member or a revered guest. It's quite common among Lebanese people to have a formal sit-down dinner that is a barbecue; you just do the cooking outside and then bring the meat indoors to a table laden with a beautiful mezza spread. All of which – pickles, dips, salads and pastries – are excellent complements to a barbecue. Next to the mezza, the barbecue would probably rate as the second most popular form of dining among the Lebanese. What is important to know is that an invitation to a Lebanese barbecue calls for nothing more than your presence. You might want to bring a sweet dish or a bottle of arak, yet it is absolutely acceptable to turn up empty-handed. Lebanese hospitality being what it is, you are actually doing your host a great honour.

Barbecue Menu

Mezza: choose 3–4 dishes

Raw kibbee (see page 108)
Kibbee nayeh

Kibbee balls (see page 102)
Kbakeeb

Lamb on skewers (see page 121)
Lahem mishwee

Kafta on skewers (see page 110)
Kafta mishwee

Garlic chicken on skewers (see page 82)
Djaj mishwee bi toum

Chicken wings in garlic (see page 82)
Jawaneh bi toum

Baba ghannooj (see page 10)
Baba ghannooj

Hummus (see page 15)
Hummous bi tahini

Bread salad (see page 44)
Fattoush

Tabbouleh (see page 47)
Tabbouleh

Potato salad (see page 48)
Salatat al bataata

Sliced fresh vegetables

. . . .

Fresh fruit

Although kibbee and kafta are popular all over Lebanon, the Lebanese never used to be known as big meat-eaters. It's only on recent trips to Lebanon that I've noticed people now seem to eat meat every day. In the past, a meat dish was something we wouldn't have more than once or twice a week, in my family at least. The houses in our village didn't have refrigerators and you had to have a block of ice delivered to keep meat from spoiling. If you wished to eat meat regularly you had to go out to buy it all the time – whereas with vegetarian dishes all the ingredients you needed were growing in your garden. Nor was it usual to have meat for lunch or dinner during the winter months. Instead, we would eat a lot of beans and lentils. If meat was eaten during winter, it would be in a dish that required only a little, such as the Meat and pine nut pastries on page 34, the Open meat and tomato pies on page 32 or the Rolled vine leaves on page 130.

Lamb is traditionally the meat used in Lebanese recipes. I use lean backstraps in the restaurant; you can also use the meat from a leg of lamb, but be sure to remove any fat or sinew. Lamb is recommended with all the meat recipes that follow, however you can substitute lean beef if you prefer – with the exception of Raw kibbee – because beef is not as tasty as lamb or goat when eaten raw.

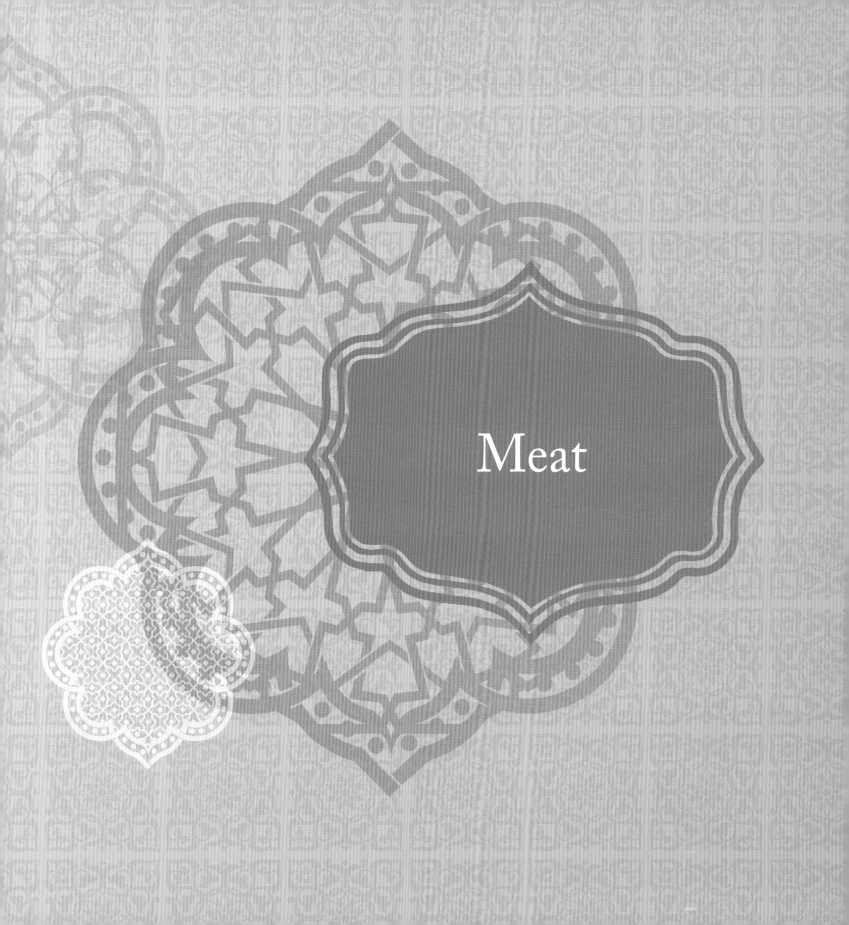

Meat

KIBBEE

Kibbee is considered Lebanon's national dish. Although it is very common and uncomplicated in many respects, with its simple combination of ingredients, it is a very special dish nonetheless. I will never forget the first time I made kibbee in Australia, two weeks after I arrived. In those days you couldn't buy an electric meat mincer, so I used a mincer operated by hand. It may sound strange to many of you, but even a meat mincer operated by hand was something novel to me. Back home in Lebanon we used the *jirin* and *modaqqa* – basically a large stone or marble mortar with a heavy wooden pestle – and the meat would be pounded until it was finely ground. Of course, electric mincers have cut the preparation time for kibbee to a fraction of what it once was. I'd probably never go back to the old way of preparing it, and yet in my home I keep with pride an old jirin and modaqqa that my mother-in-law, Latiffe, brought to Australia way back in the 1930s. Kibbee can be served raw (*kibbee nayeh*, see page 108) or cooked – the proportion of burghul to lamb changes depending on which version you make. All kibbee dishes are suitable additions to the mezza table.

Basic kibbee

If you have any kibbee mixture left over from the recipes, make small patties, then fry or bake them until cooked through. They make a simple and delicious snack served alone or with a garden salad.

1¼ cups (200 g) fine burghul (see page 214)
350 g very lean lamb fillets
piece of onion sliced from the edge of the bulb,
    about 1 cm at its widest, chopped
4 mint leaves
3 teaspoons salt
½ teaspoon freshly ground black pepper
½ teaspoon ground allspice

Wash the burghul thoroughly and drain well. Place in a bowl and set aside for 30 minutes before using.

Place the meat in a blender and mince it finely, almost to a paste. With the motor running, add the onion and mint leaves as you mince. Transfer the mixture to a mixing bowl.

Place a small bowl of water next to the mixing bowl to keep your hands moist while kneading the kibbee (this prevents it from sticking to your hands). Add the burghul to the minced meat and knead together. Add the salt, pepper and allspice and continue kneading until the mixture is well combined. Use as desired in the following kibbee recipes.

Filling for kibbee

The mixture for kibbee filling is basically the same as the Basic kibbee mixture (see page 100), except that it includes pine nuts and sumac and is prepared differently. The Basic kibbee mixture and Filling for kibbee are almost always used together – they are like two sides of the one coin.

350 g coarsely minced lean lamb
1 large onion, finely chopped
½ teaspoon salt
¼ teaspoon freshly ground black pepper
¼ teaspoon ground allspice
¼ teaspoon ground sumac (see page 215)
2 teaspoons butter
⅓ cup (50 g) pine nuts

Cook the minced lamb in a saucepan in its own juices over medium heat for 15–18 minutes, mashing with a wooden spoon to separate any lumps and stirring regularly to prevent sticking. Add the onion, salt and spices.

While the mince is browning, melt the butter in a small saucepan over medium heat, add the pine nuts and cook for 2–3 minutes or until golden brown, stirring constantly to prevent burning. Add the pine nuts to the mince mixture and continue to cook, stirring occasionally, for 20 minutes or until the mince is thoroughly cooked. Transfer to a bowl and leave to cool, then use as desired in the following recipes.

Kibbee balls »

Kbakeeb

Makes about 18
Suitable for mezza

Kibbee balls are as popular in Lebanese restaurants as they are in the home – and justly so, for they are delightful morsels for a mezza selection, and perfect when served with Hummus (see page 15), Baba ghanooj (see page 10), Yoghurt dip (see page 12) or Tahini sauce (see page 19).

1 quantity Basic kibbee (see page 100)
1 quantity Filling for kibbee (see opposite)
olive oil, for deep-frying (optional)
natural yoghurt, to serve

Dip your hands in cold water to prevent the mixture from sticking and take a small amount of the basic kibbee mixture (about the size of a golf ball) in the palm of your hand. Dip your index finger in water and insert it into the centre of the ball, turning the ball in your palm to hollow out the centre and form a long even cup.

Place 1 teaspoon of filling in the hollow, then press the top of the cup together to seal. Use the palms of your hands to shape the kibbee into a slightly elongated 'egg'-shape (see opposite). Repeat with the remaining kibbee and filling mixture.

Deep-fry the balls in a frying pan or deep-fryer of hot oil until golden and cooked through. Alternatively, place on a lightly greased baking tray and bake at 210°C for 30 minutes or grill on a barbecue. Serve hot with yoghurt.

« Baked kibbee with onion and pine nuts

Kibbee busta

Serves 6–8
Suitable for mezza

This is an even simpler version of the Baked kibbee opposite that can be made very quickly – an easy recipe for beginners. Using a round baking tin makes it easier to spread the kibbee prior to cooking.

1 cup (250 ml) olive oil
¼ cup (40 g) pine nuts
2 onions, finely sliced
½ quantity Basic kibbee (see page 100)
natural yoghurt, to serve

Preheat the oven to 210°C.

Heat ¼ cup (60 ml) of the olive oil in a frying pan over medium heat. Cook the pine nuts for 3–4 minutes or until golden brown, stirring constantly to prevent burning. Remove with a slotted spoon, then drain on paper towel. Discard some oil, then add the onion and sauté over medium heat for 4–5 minutes or until translucent. Remove from the heat immediately, then drain and mix with the pine nuts.

Place the onion mixture in the centre of a lightly greased 30 cm round baking tin. Using your hands, spread the basic kibbee mixture evenly over the onion mixture, spreading to cover the base of the tin. (This is easier if you make small patties, place them close together over the filling, then smooth the surface, dipping your hands in cold water to prevent the mixture from sticking.) The onion mixture will even out. Pour the remaining olive oil over the top. Slice the kibbee into quarters, then into quarters again to make eight slices, making sure the incisions are deep. Bake for 30–35 minutes or until browned. Serve hot or cold, with yoghurt to the side.

Baked kibbee with filling

Kibbee bi sayneeyeh

Serves 6–8
Suitable for mezza

Baked kibbee is one of the myriad ways that the Lebanese love to cook kibbee, and perhaps the easiest. It is also one of the most satisfying, especially when served straight from the oven.

1 quantity Basic kibbee (see page 100)
1 quantity Filling for kibbee (see page 102)
⅓ cup (80 ml) olive oil
natural yoghurt and salad (optional), to serve

Preheat the oven to 200°C and grease a baking tray.

Spread half of the basic kibbee mixture evenly onto the tray, followed by an even layer of the filling mixture. Press the remaining basic kibbee mixture on top of this. (This is easier if you make small patties, place them close together over the filling, then smooth the surface, dipping your hands in cold water to prevent the mixture from sticking.)

Slice the kibbee on the diagonal into diamond shapes. Pour the olive oil over the top and run a knife around the edges to prevent the kibbee from sticking to the tray. Bake for 40–45 minutes. Serve with yoghurt and, if you like, a freshly made salad.

Kibbee in yoghurt

Kibbee bi laban

Makes 6–8
Suitable for mezza

There are more than fifty different ways to cook
kibbee and, because all kibbee is made with the
finest quality lamb (which is always well seasoned),
there is rarely one version that outstrips another.
That being said, I must admit that this version,
served with a fragrant yoghurt sauce, would have
to rank highly in its popularity among the Lebanese.
If the yoghurt mixture thickens too much, add
½ cup (125 ml) boiling water to thin it down.

1 quantity Basic kibbee (see page 100)
1 quantity Filling for kibbee (see page 102)
1 cup (250 ml) boiling water
1 teaspoon dried mint
3 cloves garlic (optional)
1¼ teaspoons salt (optional)
1 teaspoon butter (optional)

Sauce
750 g natural yoghurt
1 egg
1 tablespoon plain flour, sifted
2 cups (500 ml) boiling water
⅓ cup (65 g) long-grain rice,
   washed and drained
1 teaspoon salt

Dip your hands in cold water to prevent the mixture from
sticking and take a small amount of the basic kibbee mixture
(about the size of a golf ball) in the palm of your hand.
Dip your index finger in water and insert it into the centre
of the ball, turning the ball in your palm to hollow out the
centre and form a long even cup.

Place 1 teaspoon of filling in the hollow, then press the top of
the cup together to seal. Use the palms of your hands to shape
the kibbee into a slightly elongated 'egg'-shape (see page 103).
Repeat with the remaining kibbee and filling mixture.

To make the sauce, place the yoghurt in a large saucepan,
break in the egg, then add the flour and whisk together.
Bring to the boil over medium heat, stirring constantly –
do not cover the saucepan. While stirring, gradually pour in
the boiling water. Add the rice and salt and continue to stir,
then cook for 2–3 minutes.

Add the kibbee balls to the yoghurt mixture. Add the
boiling water and dried mint. (If you wish to include garlic,
crush the garlic cloves with the salt. Melt the butter in
a small saucepan over high heat and cook the garlic for
1–2 minutes or until golden brown, then add to the pan
with the kibbee balls.) Cook for another 20 minutes or so,
then serve immediately.

Kibbee balls with labnee filling

Makes about 18
Suitable for mezza

I truly cannot recall what inspired me to come up with a labnee (drained yoghurt) filling for kibbee balls; I suspect it was the thought that if kibbee is great served with yoghurt then why not go a step further and put it inside the kibbee? What I do clearly recall is that my family and friends were pleasantly surprised the first time I served these up.

3 cups (480 g) fine burghul (see page 214)
500 g lean lamb fillets
piece of onion sliced from the edge of the bulb, about 1 cm at its widest, chopped
4 mint leaves
½ teaspoon ground allspice
½ teaspoon freshly ground black pepper
1 tablespoon salt
1 cup (250 ml) olive oil
Homemade yoghurt (see page 176) or natural yoghurt and salad, to serve

Filling
500 g Yoghurt dip (see page 12)
2 spring onions, finely chopped (¼ cup)
1 tablespoon finely chopped mint
¼ cup flat-leaf parsley, finely chopped
¼ teaspoon ground allspice
¼ teaspoon freshly ground black pepper
1 teaspoon salt
¼ teaspoon hot paprika (optional)

To prepare the kibbee casing, soak the burghul in water for 10 minutes, then drain. Finely mince the lamb meat in a blender, almost to a paste. Add the onion and mint as you mince. Transfer the mixture to a bowl, and place a small bowl of water nearby to keep your hands moist to prevent the mixture sticking. Add the burghul to the minced meat and knead together. Add the allspice, pepper and salt and continue kneading until well combined. Set aside.

To make the filling, place all the ingredients in a bowl and mix together well.

In preparation for filling the kibbee, sit a tablespoon in a bowl of water. Always remember to return the spoon to the bowl after each kibbee ball is filled – this way, the filling will slide easily into the casing.

Dip your hands in cold water to prevent the mixture from sticking and take a small amount of the basic kibbee mixture (about the size of a golf ball) in the palm of your hand. Dip your index finger in water and insert it into the centre of the ball, turning the ball in your palm to hollow out the centre and form a long even cup.

Place 1 teaspoon of filling in the hollow, then press the top of the cup together to seal. Use the palms of your hands to shape the kibbee into a slightly elongated 'egg'-shape (see page 103). Repeat with the remaining kibbee and filling mixture.

Heat the oil in a frying pan over high heat. When the oil is very hot, reduce the heat to medium and add the kibbee balls in batches. Cook for 2–3 minutes on each side or until nicely browned. Remove with a slotted spoon and drain on paper towel. Serve hot with yoghurt and salad.

Raw kibbee

Kibbee nayeh

Serves 6
Suitable for mezza

Whenever you are invited to share a meal in a Lebanese home, you can be sure you will be served *kibbee nayeh*. I cherish in my mind the many days back in Lebanon when the sound of the pounding of kibbee could be heard echoing throughout the streets. If my mother was making this and a Lebanese neighbour happened to drop in, the neighbour was rarely surprised – the pounding sound was a dead giveaway for what she was up to. The meat is pounded and served raw but without a hint of sinew and it is prepared in such a way that it is the texture of pâté when served.

1½ cups (240 g) fine burghul (see page 214)
1 kg lean lamb fillets, fat and sinew removed,
    cut into cubes
5 mint leaves
piece of onion sliced from the edge of the bulb,
    about 1 cm at its widest
2 teaspoons salt
½ teaspoon freshly ground black pepper
½ teaspoon ground allspice
fresh mint sprigs, to garnish
olive oil, Lebanese bread (see page 24,
    or purchased), sliced white onion and
    thinly sliced spring onion, to serve

Wash the burghul and leave to drain for at least 30 minutes before using.

Place the meat, mint leaves and onion in a food processor and process until the mixture forms a paste. Keeping a bowl of cold water at hand, place the meat paste in a large bowl and add the burghul, salt, pepper and allspice. Dip your hands in the water and knead the mixture, wetting your hands occasionally (to prevent the mixture from sticking) until it is combined.

Place the mixture in the centre of a large platter and mould it into an oval shape with your hands. Using a spoon, create a ridged pattern down the centre and sides. Garnish with sprigs of fresh mint and serve immediately.

To eat, spread a portion of raw kibbee evenly on your plate. Pour a little olive oil over, then tear off a piece of Lebanese bread and use it to pick up the meat. Add onion slices, spring onion and mint to taste.

KAFTA

Kibbee (see pages 100–109) might be the national dish of Lebanon, but kafta would have to run a close second. It has almost as many cooking methods as kibbee, but the most popular one is to mould it around a skewer and cook it on an open grill. Every Middle Eastern country has its own version of kafta, also called kofta, kufte and kofte. Like kibbee, the ways to cook kafta should only be limited by your imagination.

Basic kafta mixture (Kafta on skewers)

Kafta mishwee

Makes 20 skewers
Suitable for mezza

This basic recipe is a good start for those making kafta for the first time. This mixture can also be shaped into patties and cooked as you would a hamburger. Leftover mixture can be used to make the quick snack, kafta on bread (*kafta bi khoubiz*). Split a piece of Lebanese bread in half and spread evenly with a very thin layer of kafta. Bake at 180°C or place under a medium grill for 4–5 minutes. The kafta will be cooked when the bread is toasted.

1 large onion, finely chopped
2½ teaspoons salt
1 teaspoon ground allspice
1 teaspoon freshly ground black pepper
1 kg finely minced lean lamb
2 cups finely chopped flat-leaf parsley
Hummus (see page 15), to serve

Garnish
1 onion, cut in half and very finely sliced
½ cup chopped flat-leaf parsley
1 tablespoon ground sumac (see page 215)

Combine the onion, salt and spices in a large bowl. Add the meat and parsley and mix together thoroughly. Roll the mixture into twenty sausage shapes and place the pieces on 20 metal skewers. Cook on a barbecue or in a chargrill pan or frying pan over high heat for 4–5 minutes, turning to brown on all sides. Sprinkle with the garnish and serve with hummus.

Kafta with rice

Kafta bi riz

Serves 6–8

Here is another version of kafta that is extremely easy to make, but not short on taste. The addition of rice makes it great for feeding a large family.

1 quantity Basic kafta mixture (see previous page)
2 teaspoons olive oil
2 onions, halved and sliced
¼ cup (70 g) tomato paste
Lebanese rice (see page 158), to serve

Using your hands, form the kafta mixture into 2–3 cm balls. Dip your hands in cold water to prevent the meat sticking, if necessary.

Heat the oil in a saucepan over high heat and sauté the onion for 4 minutes or until lightly browned. Add the kafta balls and tomato paste and pour in enough water to cover. Bring to the boil, then reduce the heat to low and simmer, covered, for 20 minutes. Serve with Lebanese rice.

Baked kafta with potato and tomato

Kafta bi sayneeyeh

Serves 6–8

It is amazing what a little tomato paste dissolved in water can do. In this recipe, it marinates the potatoes and meat while they cook and it keeps the whole dish deliciously juicy.

1 quantity Basic kafta mixture (see previous page)
3 large potatoes, cut into 2–3 mm-thick slices
4 large tomatoes, sliced
2 tablespoons tomato paste, mixed with
    1½ cups (375 ml) water
steamed rice, to serve (optional)

Preheat the oven to 180°C. Lightly grease a baking dish.

Shape the kafta mixture into round patties, dipping your hands in cold water to prevent the meat sticking.

Stack a row of patties on an angle in the baking dish so they are leaning against the side of the dish. Pack a row of potato slices against them, also on an angle, then a row of tomato slices. Repeat if there is room and you have sufficient ingredients. Pour on the tomato paste mixture and bake for 30–40 minutes. Serve hot on a bed of steamed rice, if desired.

Baked kafta rolls with egg filling

Kafta bi bayd

Serves 6–8

This recipe leaps from my memory as a favourite family meal when I was a girl in Lebanon. The addition of hard-boiled eggs was one of the ways my mother would stretch the kafta mixture to feed a hungry family. To cook this on the stovetop, place the mixture in a lightly greased, heavy-based frying pan, cover with a lid and cook over medium heat for 10–15 minutes on each side.

1 kg finely minced lean lamb
1 teaspoon freshly ground black pepper
1 teaspoon ground allspice
2½ teaspoons salt
4–5 hard-boiled eggs, shelled
2 tablespoons olive oil
mashed potato, to serve

Garnish
1 onion, halved and very finely sliced
½ cup freshly chopped flat-leaf parsley
1 tablespoon ground sumac (see page 215)

Preheat the oven to 220°C.

Mix together the meat, spices and salt, then flatten the mixture out to form a 26 cm round on a chopping board dampened with a little water to prevent the mixture from sticking. Place the whole eggs in a line down the centre and roll the meat over, folding in the sides to completely enclose the eggs (you may need to also dampen your hands with water to prevent the meat sticking). When rolled, the kafta should resemble a meatloaf.

Alternatively, to make four smaller rolls (see opposite), take a quarter of the mince mixture and flatten it out on the board to resemble a medium-sized pizza base. Place 1 egg down the centre, then fold the sides over to form a roll. Repeat with the remaining kafta mixture and eggs to make four rolls.

Grease a roasting tin with the oil and add the kafta, rolling it in the oil. Bake, without turning, for 30–40 minutes or until golden brown.

Transfer to a chopping board, then cut into slices. Sprinkle with the garnish and serve with mashed potato.

Kafta rolls filled with spinach, pine nuts, almonds and raisins

Kafta mashi bi sabenekh

Serves 6–8

Although this version of kafta is a little more complex, I like it just as much as the traditional ones. The filling is rich with the ingredients typical of Middle Eastern cuisine: pine nuts, almonds, raisins and allspice.

1.5 kg finely minced lean lamb
1 cup finely chopped flat-leaf parsley
2 onions, finely chopped
1½ teaspoons salt
½ teaspoon ground allspice
½ teaspoon freshly ground black pepper
olive oil, for brushing
steamed vegetables, to serve

Filling
250 g spinach, washed, drained and coarsely chopped
8 spring onions, finely chopped (1½ cups)
1½ tablespoons olive oil
½ cup (80 g) pine nuts
½ cup (80 g) blanched almonds, halved
½ cup (80 g) raisins
¼ teaspoon ground allspice
¼ teaspoon finely ground black pepper
½ teaspoon salt
1 tablespoon lemon juice

Combine all the filling ingredients in a large mixing bowl and set aside.

Place the minced lamb, parsley, onion and spices in a blender and process to combine (you may need to do this in batches).

Dampen a chopping board with a little cold water to prevent the mince from sticking. Take a quarter of the mince mixture and flatten it out on the board to resemble a medium-sized pizza base. Place a quarter of the filling in a line down the centre, then fold the sides over to form a roll. Repeat with the remaining kafta mixture and filling to make four rolls.

Brush a large roasting tin or frying pan with about 2 tablespoons oil, then add the kafta rolls and cover with a lid. Gently cook over medium heat for 15–20 minutes on both sides, or until nicely browned (the total cooking time should be 30–40 minutes). Alternatively, preheat the oven to 220°C and pour the oil into a roasting tin. Add the kafta rolls and turn to coat in the oil, then bake for 30–40 minutes without turning.

Transfer to a chopping board, then cut into slices (see page 113). Serve hot with steamed vegetables.

Latiffe's rabbit casserole

Yakhanet aarnab

Serves 6

My husband, John, loved to eat rabbit, either farmed or wild, and in whatever manner it was cooked – roasted, grilled, pan-fried or braised. His mother, Latiffe, indulged his love of rabbit and this recipe was one of her specialties, which she kindly handed down to me as it was one of John's favourites. You may need to order a rabbit from your local butcher – if so, ask for a young rabbit as the meat is both delicate and flavourful.

2 rabbits, chopped in half widthways
2 cinnamon sticks or bay leaves
½ cup (125 ml) olive oil
3 onions, halved and sliced
¼ cup tomato paste mixed with
   2 cups (500 ml) water
2 teaspoons salt
½ teaspoon white pepper
½ teaspoon ground allspice
¼ teaspoon hot paprika (optional)
Lebanese rice (see page 158), to serve

Place the rabbit in a large heavy-based saucepan, cover with water, then add 1 of the cinnamon sticks or bay leaves and bring to the boil. Reduce the heat to low and simmer for 5–10 minutes, then drain and rinse the rabbit under cold running water (this helps remove the gamey aroma).

Return the rabbit to the pan with clean water and the remaining cinnamon stick or bay leaf, cover with a lid and bring to the boil again. Reduce the heat to low and simmer for 40–45 minutes or until the meat comes off the bone. Drain and set aside to cool, then tear the meat from the bones. Discard the bones and set the meat aside.

Meanwhile, heat the oil in a flameproof casserole dish over high heat and sauté the onion for 6–7 minutes or until golden brown. Add the tomato paste mixture and cook, covered, for 5 minutes. Stir in the salt, pepper and allspice and cook, covered, for another 5 minutes. Add the rabbit meat and hot paprika (if using). Check the consistency and, if the sauce has already thickened, add another ½ cup (125 ml) water to thin if necessary. Cover and cook over low heat for 30 minutes or until the sauce is reduced and thickened, stirring regularly.

Serve with Lebanese rice.

Stuffed whole lamb

Qouzi

Serves 16

This magnificent dish is made to feed a large crowd on special occasions, such as christenings, weddings or Christmas lunch. A whole lamb is required and these can be hard to obtain. My advice is to go to a good butcher well in advance of when you want to make the dish, and ask them to order the smallest whole lamb they can get for you. Oh, and you will also need an oven large enough to fit the lamb. To produce a delicious glaze, smear natural yoghurt over the lamb for the last fifteen minutes of cooking.

1 × 8–9 kg whole lamb
2 potatoes or carrots
salads and pan-fried vegetables, to serve

Stuffing
500 g coarsely minced lean lamb
1 tablespoon light olive oil
1½ cups (235 g) pine nuts
1½ cups (210 g) slivered almonds
6 cups (1.2 kg) long-grain rice,
  washed and drained
1 tablespoon salt
2 teaspoons freshly ground black pepper
2 teaspoons ground allspice

To make the stuffing, brown the minced lamb in a saucepan in its own juices over medium heat for 10–12 minutes, mashing with a wooden spoon to separate the lumps and stirring frequently to prevent sticking.

Preheat the oven to 220°C.

Meanwhile, heat the oil in a frying pan and sauté the pine nuts and almonds over medium heat for 2–3 minutes or until golden brown, stirring constantly to prevent burning. Remove the nuts with a slotted spoon and drain on paper towel, then stir into the pan of browned mince. Add the rice, salt, pepper and allspice and reduce the heat to low. Stir in 1 cup (250 ml) water and cook for 5 minutes. The rice will not be completely cooked.

Stuff the lamb with the rice mixture and sew up with strong cotton, placing 1 potato or carrot at each end to leave an opening. Place the lamb in a large roasting tin, pour in ½ cup (125 ml) water and cover completely with foil. Roast for 30 minutes. Remove 1 potato or carrot and pour another cup water into the rice mixture in the lamb – this will cook the rice in the stuffing. Replace the potato or carrot and foil and return the lamb to the oven. Reduce the temperature to 180°C and roast for 1 hour. Once again, remove 1 potato or carrot and pour another cup water into the rice mixture in the lamb. Replace the potato or carrot and foil and roast for a further 1 hour. Remove the foil and roast for 15–20 minutes, basting occasionally with the pan juices, until the lamb is golden brown and cooked through.

Serve warm or at room temperature on a large platter with a selection of freshly made salads or pan-fried vegetables.

Lamb on skewers

Lahem mishwee

Serves 10–12

My husband, John, used to organise barbecues at picnic grounds in and around Melbourne. I remember that on most of these occasions other picnickers would gather around with genuine curiosity when I started placing lamb or chicken skewers on the barbecue. My children couldn't understand what the fuss was about! To them it was just a normal barbecue, but for the Australian onlookers it was completely foreign. Needless to say, we always ended up with a much larger gathering than intended.

1.5 kg lean lamb fillets, cut into 3–4 cm cubes
½ teaspoon freshly ground black pepper
½ teaspoon ground allspice
1 teaspoon salt
1 tablespoon olive oil
3 onions, quartered

Garnish
1 onion, halved and very finely sliced
½ cup freshly chopped flat-leaf parsley
1 tablespoon ground sumac (see page 215)

Mix the meat with the pepper, allspice, salt and oil. Cover and leave to marinate for at least 1 hour.

Thread 5–6 marinated lamb cubes onto metal skewers, alternating with an onion piece between every second cube or so. Cook on a hot barbecue or under a hot griller for 5–7 minutes or until cooked to your liking.

Mix together the garnish ingredients. Serve immediately with the garnish to the side.

CHRISTMAS

For the Lebanese, Christmas preparations start a week or two in advance of the big day, and I'm not talking about making sure you've ordered a turkey or a glazed ham. This is a time spent preparing generous platters laden with traditional sweets, nougats and sugared almonds. That's because traditionally, from Christmas morning right through to New Year's Day and several days beyond, there will be a constant stream of people dropping in and it's imperative to have sweets to offer to your guests along with coffee or a liqueur. Christmas lunch is, of course, the most important meal of the season and a Lebanese Christmas shares the same general characteristics of Christmas celebrations all around the world. The main difference is in the type of foods served. Rather than, say, roast turkey, ham and fruit mince pies, a typical Lebanese Christmas lunch would include a Stuffed whole lamb (see page 118), Chicken and rice (see page 84), a serving of fish such as Baked fish with tahini and spicy filling (see page 66) or Fish and rice (see page 69), along with Kibbee (see pages 100–108), and most definitely a mezza spread. As in other cultures, Christmas is a unifying experience for the Lebanese, a time for us to give gifts as a symbol of our goodwill to others. As far as I am concerned, for Christmas there is no greater gift than the gift of food, and regardless of who we are or where we come from, when you sit at my table we are all one people.

Christmas Lunch

Set up a special table or tray with arak, liqueurs, sugared almonds and a selection of nougats and chocolates, to be offered to guests. As many people will visit the household during this period, keep the tray well stocked until after the New Year.

Mezza: choose 3–4 dishes

Dried figs, nuts and sultanas

Tabbouleh (see page 47)
Tabbouleh

Raw kibbee (see page 108)
Kibbee nayeh

Stuffed whole lamb (see page 118)
Qouzi

Rolled vine leaves (see page 130)
Ma'hshi warak enib

Chicken and rice (see page 84)
Djaj a riz

Stuffed marrows (see page 135)
Ma'hshi koussa

. . . .

Fresh fruit

. . . .

Lebanese coffee *Ahawe* (see page 212)

. . . .

Selection from, or one of:

Baklava (see page 202)
Baklawa

Sweet cheese with syrup (see page 211)
Halawat el jibeen

Lebanese shortbread (see page 195)
Ghraybi

Semolina slice (see page 199)
Nummoora

Walnut-filled pancakes (see page 206)
Atoyif

Sweet ladies' fingers (see page 201)
Zund el sit

One of the virtues of Lebanese home cooking is the delightful balance of meat, vegetables, grains and spices. Popular vegetables are those with leaves – cabbage, spinach, silver beet or vine leaves. You will notice that these dishes tend to feature a higher ratio of vegetables to meat. The quantity of meat used in Lebanon isn't large, and rice, which is called for in almost all of the recipes in this chapter, is relatively inexpensive – which is another reason for the popularity of these dishes, especially among villagers. They are also popular because these vegetable and meat dishes can be easily adapted to become Lenten dishes (recipes free of meat or dairy foods), which is appropriate for times when Lebanese people are observing periods of fasting.

In Lebanon it is not traditional for meat to be eaten everyday in large quantities, yet when invited to a Lebanese meal it is likely you will be served a variety of dishes built on modest combinations of meat and vegetables. They are not at all heavy but are as nutritious as they are delicious. The modesty of these dishes is significant because when you are invited to sit at a Lebanese table you are considered part of the family and will be shown the same respect as a family member. On that note, this chapter is dedicated to your health!

Vegetable &
Meat Dishes

VINE LEAVES

Vine leaves have been used to wrap food for centuries and, throughout the Middle East, serving them is considered a token of gracious living. In Lebanon no mezza table is complete without them. Two kinds of vine leaves may be used in most recipes that call for them: fresh and pickled.

My neighbours in Australia have always known of my preference for fresh, tender leaves. They have kept me in steady supply by picking their own vines, and have even sought out the vines of other people. It is always better to use small, young, fresh leaves, for they are tender and have a stronger flavour; they are also the perfect size for rolling. Pickled vine leaves can be bought from any Middle Eastern grocery store, specialist delis and sometimes from larger supermarkets. They are preserved in salted water, so they require extensive washing and should be tasted before use. Do not add salt when you cook with them as they are salty enough.

Preserved or pickled vine leaves

Warak enib makbous

This is not so much a recipe as a method to preserve and keep vine leaves until ready to use in making Rolled vine leaves (see page 130). We do this because fresh young and tender leaves are not available all year round. The purest way to preserve vine leaves is to pack them firmly in an airtight container and put them in the freezer. I prefer to preserve or pickle meal-sized quantities of vine leaves in smaller jars. After years of practice I know how much I require for a meal.

fresh vine leaves, stalks removed
water (if pickling)
1 egg (if pickling)
salt (if pickling)

To preserve vine leaves, stack them firmly on top of each other in an airtight, sterilised pickling jar (see page 215). Store in a dark place. (Use small jars to preserve enough leaves for one meal. Once a jar is open the leaves must be used immediately.) To store vine leaves in the freezer, place the thoroughly dry leaves in a plastic container. Use within 2 months and allow 5–8 minutes for them to thaw before using.

To pickle vine leaves, wash the leaves thoroughly and soak in water overnight. Wash again the next morning and drain, reserving the water. Place the leaves in a sterilised preserving jar. Put a raw, unbroken egg in the reserved water and add salt until the egg floats to the top: this indicates you have used the right amount of salt! Remove the egg and add the salty water to the jar. Seal and store in a dark place. You can use the leaves after a few weeks, just remove what you need and reseal. Use within 2 months.

Rolled vine leaves

Ma'hshi warak enib

Suitable for mezza

Ma'hshi warak enib is the most popular of the Lebanese repertoire of vegetable and meat dishes, and that's because we have a lot of vines in Lebanon. As a young girl, during the months of spring I would go out to the fields carrying a huge basket to pick young and tender leaves and bring them back home to my mother. We would then wash them and lay them out nicely to dry. Because vine leaves were plentiful we could always preserve enough to see us through the seasons when the vines were bare. I remember these times as being something of a quiet ritual performed with my mother.

Patience and care are essential 'ingredients' here. It takes time to select the leaves and prepare the filling, as well as deft fingers to roll them up into slim parcels that are exactly the same size. Vine leaves are one of the jewels of the Lebanese table and great pride is taken when presenting them – as the Lebanese saying goes: 'A long time in the making and a minute in the eating'.

You can use Pickled leaves (see page 128) instead of fresh, but make sure you wash them very thoroughly to remove the salt. If you do this, omit the final teaspoon of salt sprinkled over the rolls before cooking.

For a meatier dish, line the base of the pan with lean pieces of lamb or lamb chops instead of vine leaves. For a vegetarian version, see opposite.

750 g fresh or Pickled vine leaves (see page 128), washed and drained
2 cups (300 g) long-grain rice, washed and drained
500 g coarsely minced lean lamb
1 teaspoon ground allspice
1 teaspoon freshly ground black pepper
2 teaspoons butter
1 tablespoon salt
2½ tablespoons lemon juice
natural yoghurt, to serve

If using fresh leaves, blanch in boiling water to make soft and easy to roll, then drain. If the leaves are very large, cut in half lengthways. Trim the stalks, then line the bottom of a large heavy-based saucepan with a layer of leaves.

Place the rice, lamb, spices, butter and 3 teaspoons of the salt in a bowl and mix together well. Place 1 teaspoon of the mixture on the stalk side of a leaf, centred at the base of the stalk, and spread it out for about 6 cm across the leaf. Fold the top of the leaf over the mixture, then fold in the sides and roll. Each roll should be about 1 cm in diameter and 6 cm long. (Although the leaves will vary in size, put the same amount of mixture on each.)

Place each roll in the lined saucepan, arranging them in a circular pattern. When all the leaves or mixture have been used, pour over the lemon juice and sprinkle with the remaining salt, if using. Pour in enough water to cover the rolls and place a heatproof plate on top (this will stop them opening during cooking). Cover with a lid and bring to the boil over high heat. Reduce the heat to very low and cook for 1–1½ hours, which leaves plenty of time for the rice to cook. Occasionally check that the water has not evaporated from the saucepan and top up with boiling water if necessary. Serve hot or at room temperature, with yoghurt. Leftovers will keep in a covered container in the refrigerator for up to 2 days.

Vegetarian rolled vine leaves

Ma'hshi warak enib ateygh

Suitable for mezza

One of the great things about most traditional Lebanese recipes is the ease with which they can be adapted to cater for vegetarian tastes. This recipe is a prime example of this versatility.

750 g fresh or Pickled vine leaves
   (see page 128), washed and drained
2 tomatoes, thickly sliced
¼ cup (60 ml) olive oil
juice of 1 lemon
1 teaspoon salt (optional)
natural yoghurt, to serve

Filling
1½ cups (300 g) basmati or long-grain rice,
   washed and drained
2 onions, finely chopped
2 cups finely chopped flat-leaf parsley
1 teaspoon finely chopped mint
2 teaspoons salt
¼ teaspoon ground allspice
¼ teaspoon freshly ground black pepper

Blanch the vine leaves in boiling water to make them soft and easy to roll, then drain. If the leaves are very large, cut them in half lengthways. Trim the stalks, then line the bottom of a large, heavy-based saucepan with a layer of leaves and the tomato slices.

To make the filling, combine all the ingredients in a bowl and mix together well.

Place 1 teaspoon of the filling mixture on the stalk side of a leaf, centred at the base of the stalk, and spread it out for about 6 cm across the leaf. Fold the top of the leaf over the mixture, then fold in the sides and roll. Each roll should be about 1 cm in diameter and 6 cm long. (Although the leaves will vary in size, put the same amount of mixture on each.)

Place each roll in the lined saucepan, arranging them in a circular pattern. When all the leaves or mixture have been used, pour over the lemon juice and sprinkle with the remaining salt, if using. Pour in enough water to cover the rolls and place a heatproof plate on top (this will stop them opening during cooking). Cover with a lid and bring to the boil over high heat. Reduce the heat to very low and cook for 1–1½ hours, which leaves plenty of time for the rice to cook. Occasionally check that the water has not evaporated from the saucepan and top up with boiling water if necessary. Serve hot or at room temperature, with yoghurt. Leftovers will keep in a covered container in the refrigerator for up to 2 days.

Cabbage rolls

Ma'hshi malfouf

Makes 25–30
Suitable for mezza

The Lebanese have a fondness for stuffed vegetables that is second to none. Cabbage rolls are another Lebanese classic and a mezza favourite. They can be served hot or cold, with fresh yoghurt or a squeeze of lemon juice. Be sure to select a flat, round cabbage: it will have fewer crinkled leaves that can be difficult to roll.

1 cabbage, outer leaves discarded
8 cloves garlic, finely chopped
3 tomatoes, finely chopped
3 teaspoons dried mint
¼ cup (60 ml) lemon juice,
   plus extra to serve (optional)

Filling
2 cups (400 g) long-grain rice,
   washed and drained
500 g coarsely minced lean lamb
1 teaspoon freshly ground black pepper
1 teaspoon ground allspice
3 teaspoons salt
20 g butter

Garnish (optional)
1 small tomato, finely chopped
1 clove garlic, finely chopped

Remove the core of the cabbage, cutting as deep as possible into the cabbage. With the hollow centre down, submerge the cabbage in a large saucepan of boiling water. Remove individual leaves as they soften and break away and place in a colander to drain. Set aside a few leaves to line the pan.

Spread the remaining leaves on a chopping board and cut in half lengthways, removing the centre stalk. Cut in half again widthways, trimming to shape the leaves into 8 cm × 11 cm rectangles – don't worry if not all the leaves are evenly sized. Set aside the cabbage trimmings to make Pan-fried cabbage (see page 173), if desired.

To make the filling, combine all the filling ingredients in a bowl and mix together well. Take 1 heaped teaspoon of the filling and pile it along the top of a quartered cabbage leaf, allowing a little space on both sides, then roll (there is no need to fold in the edges). Squeeze the roll firmly in the palm of your hand to remove any excess water. Repeat until all the filling is used.

Line the base of a medium-sized heavy-based saucepan with the reserved cabbage leaves. Pack the rolls close together in the pan, but do not press down or pack them too firmly. When a layer is completed, sprinkle with a little garlic and tomato and 1 teaspoon of the dried mint (there should be three layers). Repeat until all the rolls are in the pan.

Pour lemon juice over the rolls and add enough water to cover. Place a heatproof plate over the rolls to prevent them from breaking apart while cooking. Cover and bring to the boil over high heat, then reduce the heat to low and cook, covered, for 1 hour or until the rice is cooked. Serve hot with a squeeze of lemon juice, or garnish with chopped tomato and garlic, if desired.

Stuffed marrows

Ma'hshi koussa

Makes 12

Ma'hshi koussa are a personal favourite of mine. *Koussa*, or baby marrows, are readily available today, sometimes sold as Lebanese zucchini or white zucchini. Back in the 1950s they were not grown commercially in Australia. To make the dish we had to resort to using the dark-green zucchini. My uncle Joe brought back some koussa seeds from Lebanon when he returned after a brief visit, and he shared them with many in the community. It wasn't long before we started eating 'real' ma'hshi koussa again.

You can buy a utensil called a *manakra* from Middle Eastern food stores to remove the pulp (that is, flesh) from marrows. Otherwise, a corer or a thin, sharp knife will do the job just as well.

To make the variation known as *koussa bi laban* (stuffed marrows with yoghurt sauce) cook the marrows in a saucepan of water without adding the tomato paste or salt, then remove from heat and drain. Make the Yoghurt sauce on page 106, but omit the rice and only boil for 15 minutes. Submerge the drained marrows in the hot sauce and serve.

To make this dish suitable for vegetarians, stuff the marrows with the filling for Silverbeet rolls on page 146.

12 small (10–15 cm long) marrows (Lebanese zucchini)
2¼ teaspoons salt
2 heaped tablespoons tomato paste
natural yoghurt, to serve (optional)

Filling
1 cup (200 g) long-grain rice, washed and drained
250 g coarsely minced lean lamb
½ teaspoon ground allspice
½ teaspoon freshly ground black pepper
2 teaspoons salt
2 teaspoons butter, melted
1 small tomato, finely chopped

Wash the marrows thoroughly under running water. Cut off the stalks and the very tops of the marrows. Remove and discard a sliver from the hard ends (the marrows need to be intact). Carefully hollow out the pulp (flesh) using a corer or small, sharp knife, leaving a 5 mm-thick shell. (Reserve the pulp for another recipe, such as the omelettes on page 151). Place 1 teaspoon of the salt in a bowl of water and wash the marrows – this will keep them firm while they cook. Drain and set aside.

To make the filling, mix the ingredients and 1 tablespoon water in a bowl well. Stuff each marrow with the mixture, leaving a 2 cm gap at the top. It's best to do this with your hands, shaking the marrows and lightly pressing the mixture down into the centre as you go. Roll any leftover filling into one or two balls and place in the saucepan with the marrows.

Place the marrows in a large saucepan and cover completely with water. Add the tomato paste and remaining salt and bring to the boil over high heat. Reduce the heat to low and cook for 45 minutes. The marrows should be tender but not break apart when removed from the pan. Serve hot with yoghurt, if desired.

Baked stuffed potatoes

Ma'hshi bataata

Makes 7

The humble potato need not always play second fiddle to a main dish – with a little creativity and devotion it can be turned into an excellent substantial meal in itself. Frying the potato shells before baking not only reduces the baking time, it also gives the potatoes an attractive honey-coloured finish. This part of the recipe can be skipped if preferred; just remember that you'll need to increase the baking time by about twenty minutes.

7 large potatoes, peeled (any variety will do)
½ cup (125 ml) olive oil
1 large tomato, cut into large cubes
¼ cup (70 g) tomato paste, mixed with
   2–3 cups (500–750 ml) water,
   depending on size of baking dish
1 teaspoon salt (optional)

Filling
300 g coarsely minced lean lamb
½ onion, finely chopped
1 teaspoon salt
½ teaspoon ground allspice
1 tablespoon lemon juice, pomegranate molasses
   (see page 215) or ground sumac (see page 215)
20 g butter
½ cup (80 g) pine nuts

Cleanly cut off a small slice at each end of the potatoes so they stand upright. Reserve the ends for later use. Using a corer or sharp knife, make an opening at one end and hollow out the inside of each potato, taking care not to pierce through to the outside. The shell of each potato should be about 5 mm thick. Set aside the potato flesh for later.

Heat the oil in a large frying pan over high heat. Carefully add the potato shells and cook for about 5 minutes on each side until golden brown. Remove and drain on paper towel, open-end down.

Preheat the oven to 250°C. To make the filling, cook the minced lamb in a saucepan over medium heat for 10–12 minutes in its own juices until browned, mashing with a wooden spoon to separate any lumps and stirring frequently to prevent sticking. Add the onion, salt, allspice and lemon juice, pomegranate molasses or sumac. Stir to combine and cook for another 5 minutes.

Meanwhile, melt the butter in a small saucepan over medium heat and cook the pine nuts for 2–3 minutes or until golden, stirring constantly to prevent burning. Add the pine nuts and melted butter to the lamb mixture and stir to combine.

Fill each potato with the lamb mixture. Select seven of the tomato cubes to use as tops, then press one piece firmly into the opening of each potato. Finely chop the remaining tomato. Layer the reserved potato flesh and bases and finely chopped tomato in the bottom of a deep baking dish or earthenware casserole, then place the stuffed potatoes in the dish, keeping them upright as best you can. Pour the tomato paste mixture over the top and sprinkle with salt if desired. Bake for 45–60 minutes or until tender. Serve immediately.

Spinach with meat

Sabanekh a lahem

Serves 6–8

This is a familiar and simple Middle Eastern dish – and very nutritious too!

650 g coarsely minced lean lamb
2 onions, finely chopped
20 g butter
1 teaspoon salt
½ teaspoon ground allspice
½ teaspoon freshly ground black pepper
¼ cup (40 g) pine nuts (optional)
2 tablespoons olive oil (optional)
2 bunches spinach, washed and stalks removed,
   leaves roughly chopped
2 tablespoons lemon juice
natural yoghurt and Lebanese rice (see page 158),
   to serve

If using the pine nuts, preheat the oven to 180°C.

Cook the minced lamb in a saucepan over medium heat for 8–10 minutes in its own juices until browned, mashing with a wooden spoon to separate any lumps and stirring frequently to prevent sticking. Add the onion, butter, salt and spices and cook, stirring, for another 10 minutes.

Meanwhile, toss the pine nuts and oil together (if using), then spread on a baking tray and roast in the oven for 5–6 minutes or until golden. Remove from the oven and set aside.

Add the spinach to the meat mixture and cook for 5 minutes or until the spinach has wilted. Stir in the lemon juice and pine nuts (if using). Serve with yoghurt and Lebanese rice.

Rice with chickpeas and lamb »

Riz bi dfeen

Serves 6–8

If you have never attempted to cook Lebanese food before now, then this recipe is a good place to start. The chickpeas form a base for the fragrant spices, especially the cumin, whose flavour is quite pronounced in this dish. Be sure to soak the chickpeas the night before you intend to make this dish.

½ cup (100 g) dried chickpeas, washed and drained
750 g lean lamb fillets, cut into 2 cm cubes, or 4 lamb shanks
1½ teaspoons salt
6–8 pickling onions, peeled or 2 onions, quartered
2 cups (400 g) long-grain rice, washed and drained
1 teaspoon ground cumin
½ teaspoon freshly ground black pepper
½ teaspoon ground allspice
20 g butter (optional)
natural yoghurt (optional), to serve

Cover the chickpeas with water and soak overnight. Next day, drain.

Place the meat in a saucepan with ½ teaspoon of the salt and enough water to cover. Bring to the boil over high heat, then drain and wash the meat under cold running water. Return the meat to the pan with 2 litres clean water. Cover and boil over high heat for 30 minutes. (If using lamb shanks, strip the meat from the bones and return the meat to the pan.) Add the chickpeas and onions, then reduce the heat to low and cook, covered, for 1–1½ hours or until the meat is tender. Stir in the rice, cumin, pepper, allspice and remaining salt, then cover and cook over low heat for 15–20 minutes or until the rice is cooked. Stir in the butter (if using) and serve hot with yoghurt to the side, if desired.

Eggplant casserole

Ablama

Serves 6
Suitable for mezza

Here is a recipe that bears my name, but that is not the only reason I'm fond of it. *Ablama* is a delightfully aromatic dish, rich with classic ingredients from the Lebanese kitchen – lamb, eggplant, allspice, pine nuts, and lemon or pomegranate – and perfect for the mezza table.

6 baby or Japanese eggplants
1 teaspoon salt
½ cup (125 ml) olive oil
4 tomatoes, diced or 1 × 400 g tin diced tomatoes
1 tablespoon tomato paste (optional)
steamed rice or Lebanese rice (see page 158), to serve

Filling
250 g minced lean lamb
½ onion, finely chopped
1 teaspoon salt
½ teaspoon ground allspice
1 tablespoon lemon juice, pomegranate molasses
    (see page 215) or ground sumac (see page 215)
20 g butter
½ cup (80 g) pine nuts

Trim and peel the stem and leafy sections from the eggplants, but do not remove them. Roughly peel the eggplants, then place them in water with ½ teaspoon of the salt and set aside for at least 1 hour. This prevents the eggplants from absorbing too much oil when fried.

To make the filling, cook the minced lamb in a saucepan in its own juices over medium heat for 10-12 minutes, mashing with a wooden spoon to separate any lumps and stirring frequently to prevent sticking. When the mince has browned, add the onion, salt, allspice and lemon juice, pomegranate molasses or sumac. Stir to mix and cook for another 5 minutes.

Meanwhile, melt the butter in a small saucepan over medium heat and cook the pine nuts for 2–3 minutes until golden brown, stirring constantly to prevent burning. Add the pine nuts and melted butter to the mince and stir, then remove the pan from the heat.

Drain the eggplants and pat dry with paper towel. Heat the oil in a large frying pan over high heat and cook the eggplants for about 5 minutes on each side until soft and golden brown. Remove from the pan and drain on paper towel for a minute or two. Next, butterfly the eggplants by making a careful incision along the length of each eggplant and opening them out. Place 1–2 tablespoons of the filling on one side, then fold the other side over to enclose.

Arrange the eggplants in a roasting tin and spread the tomato along the sides. Sprinkle with the remaining salt and add ½–1 cup (125–250 ml) water – just enough to cover the eggplants. (For a rich tomato flavour, dissolve the tomato paste in the water before pouring it in.) Cook the eggplants, covered, over medium heat for 10 minutes or until the eggplants are heated through. Serve with rice and some of the tomato sauce spooned over.

The Lebanese are renowned for their love of vegetables. One distinguishing feature of Middle Eastern cuisine (and Lebanese in particular) is the ease with which it can be adapted for vegetarians when called for, especially when people are observing religious customs. For example, traditional vegetable dishes are eaten throughout the Christian Lenten period as it is common to abstain from eating meat at this time. Dishes such as Lentils and rice (see page 155), Green beans in olive oil (see page 162), Felafel (see page 144), Spinach pies (see page 36) and lentil-based soups (see pages 58–62) are all popular during Lent.

Lebanese people take great care to preserve and pickle their favourite vegetables (see pages 16–21), as well as to dry them. Villagers in Lebanon today still continue to dry vegetables, no longer out of necessity but because they're sure that the home-dried vegetables will be free of preservatives and chemicals.

In the past, everyone in a Lebanese village had their own vegetable patch. This reminds me of a saying: 'If you want a meal, you'll find it in any Lebanese garden'. If anyone showed up unexpectedly my mother could make a banquet out of what she had growing in her garden.

Vegetarian

Felafel

Felafel

Makes 10–12
Suitable for mezza

Although Egyptian in origin, felafel quickly found popularity in Lebanon as a healthy street food. Soon after my restaurant opened, I took a stall at the local Lygon Street Festa and served felafel and kafta. I thought I had made enough to last the day, but I couldn't keep up with demand. Only one girl worked with me, and the poor thing had to go back to the restaurant every hour or so for more supplies so I didn't run out.

Remember that you will need to start a day in advance because chickpeas and broad beans must be soaked overnight in water before cooking. You can use a utensil called an *ol'eb felalfer* to form evenly rounded felafels. This can be purchased from any Middle Eastern food store.

1 cup (200 g) dried chickpeas, washed and drained
1 cup (180 g) dried split broad beans, washed and drained
2 teaspoons bicarbonate of soda
1 large onion, quartered
6 cloves garlic
1 cup coriander, washed (about 1 bunch)
3 red bird's eye hot chillies (more or less as preferred)
2 teaspoons salt
½ teaspoon freshly ground black pepper
½ teaspoon ground allspice
2 teaspoons ground cumin
olive oil, for deep-frying
Pickled turnips (see page 16), sliced tomato, lettuce and chopped flat-leaf parsley, to serve (optional)

Sauce
½ cup (140 g) tahini
pinch of salt
¼ cup (60 ml) lemon juice
1 small tomato, chopped
1 small Lebanese cucumber, peeled and chopped
2 tablespoons chopped flat-leaf parsley

Cover the chickpeas and broad beans with water, add 1 teaspoon of the bicarbonate of soda and soak overnight. Next day, drain, rinse and place them in a food processor with the onion, garlic, coriander and chillies. Blend until all the ingredients are well combined but still have texture. Transfer to a large bowl and mix in the salt and spices.

To make the sauce, place the tahini and salt in a bowl and slowly add the lemon juice and ¼ cup (60 ml) water, stirring continuously. Add the tomato, cucumber and parsley and stir to combine.

When you're ready to cook the felafel, add the remaining bicarbonate of soda (this allows them to rise and become light and fluffy). Form tablespoonfuls of the mixture into balls and deep-fry in batches in a frying pan of very hot oil for 2 minutes on each side or until golden brown. Drain on paper towel. (The felafel mixture does not have to be cooked immediately. To store, place in an airtight container and refrigerate for up to a week or freeze for up to a year.)

Serve hot with the sauce spooned over accompanied by sliced tomato, lettuce and pickled turnip and garnished with parsley.

Silverbeet rolls

Ma'hshi sleeq salak

Makes 25
Suitable for mezza

Abla's Restaurant had only been open a few months when I took an outside job for a charity event run by the Arab community at the Brunswick Town Hall. There were supposed to be only 250 people attending, but we ended up catering for nearly 400. I made so many silverbeet rolls that evening that the next morning my husband told me my hands had still been going through the motions of rolling the leaves when I was fast asleep! Vine leaves or cabbage leaves can be used instead of silverbeet leaves.

**2 bunches fresh, crisp silverbeet, well washed
  and drained**
½ teaspoon salt
1 tablespoon lemon juice

Filling
**½ cup (100 g) dried split chickpeas
  (available from Middle Eastern food stores),
  washed and drained**
1 cup (200 g) long-grain rice, washed and drained
3 tomatoes, chopped
1 onion, chopped
1 cup chopped flat-leaf parsley
1 tablespoon chopped mint
1 teaspoon salt
½ teaspoon ground allspice
½ teaspoon freshly ground black pepper
2 tablespoons lemon juice
⅓ cup (80 ml) olive oil

To make the filling, cover the chickpeas with water and soak overnight. Next day, drain and place in a bowl with the remaining ingredients. Mix well.

Remove the stalk ends and centre stalks of the silverbeet, reserving the ends for Silverbeet stalks with tahini and lemon juice (see page 161). Line the bottom of a large, heavy-based saucepan with any irregular-shaped leaves. Cut the other leaves into even rectangles, approximately 8 cm × 10 cm. Transfer to a clean bowl and pour hot water over to soften them.

Take 1 heaped teaspoon of the filling and pile along the top edge of a softened silverbeet rectangle, allowing a little space on both sides, and roll (there is no need to fold in the edges). Squeeze the roll firmly in the palm of your hand to remove any excess juice over a bowl, reserving the excess juice. Repeat until all the filling is used.

Place the rolls in layers in the lined saucepan. Pour the reserved juice into pan and add the salt, lemon juice and ½ cup (125 ml) water. Cover with the lid and bring to the boil over high heat, then reduce the heat to medium and cook for 30–35 minutes.

Serve immediately for best results, but they can also be served at room temperature.

Spicy peas

Bazalia

Serves 6

This easy dish is a Middle Eastern favourite. *Bazalia* is best eaten the day after making because it allows the peas to absorb all the flavours. If you wish for some variety, add 500 g chopped skinless chicken breast or thigh fillets or the same amount of coarsely minced lean lamb. Brown the meat after the onion and garlic, before adding the remaining ingredients.

1 tablespoon olive oil
1 large onion, finely chopped
1 clove garlic, sliced
3 large tomatoes, coarsely chopped
2 tablespoons tomato paste
2 teaspoons salt
½ teaspoon freshly ground black pepper
½ teaspoon ground allspice
4 cups (640 g) podded fresh peas or frozen peas
Lebanese rice (see page 158), to serve

Heat the oil in a large saucepan over high heat and sauté the onion and garlic for 4–5 minutes or until lightly browned. Add the remaining ingredients and 3 cups (750 ml) water and cover with a lid. Reduce the heat to medium and cook for 20 minutes or until the sauce has thickened and peas are tender. Serve hot with Lebanese rice.

Pumpkin kibbee »

Kibbee't el jlant

Makes about 20
Suitable for mezza

This variation on the Lebanese national dish kibbee was developed to observe the Lenten custom of abstaining from meat. It is also a Good Friday dish. The patties can also be baked at 200°C for 40 minutes. If you omit the pumpkin and double the potato, the dish is called *kibbee el bataata*. The dried split chickpeas will need to be soaked overnight before cooking.

¼ cup (50 g) dried split chickpeas (available from Middle Eastern food stores), washed and drained
500 g pumpkin, peeled and chopped (to yield 2 cups)
3 potatoes, chopped (to yield 2 cups)
1 cup (160 g) fine burghul (see page 214), washed and drained
1 onion, finely chopped
1 tablespoon finely chopped mint
2 tablespoons finely chopped flat-leaf parsley
2 tablespoons finely chopped coriander (optional)
2 teaspoons salt
½ teaspoon freshly ground black pepper
½ teaspoon ground allspice
1¼ cups (185 g) plain flour, sifted
¼ cup (60 ml) olive oil, approximately
natural yoghurt, to serve

Soak the chickpeas in water overnight. Next day, drain. Boil the pumpkin and potato in a saucepan for 15 minutes or until soft, then drain and mash. Add the chickpeas, burghul, onion, herbs, salt and spices and mix thoroughly. Add the flour and mix well. Shape into 6–7 cm patties. Heat the olive oil in a frying pan over high heat and fry in batches for 5 minutes on each side or until golden brown on the outside and soft in the centre. Remove with a slotted spoon and drain on paper towel. Serve with yoghurt.

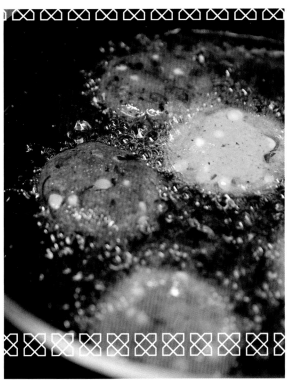

« Marrow omelettes

Ijjie

Makes 18–20 small omelettes
Suitable for mezza

These omelettes can be fried or baked and eaten hot or cold. In village life, leftovers are wrapped in bread and taken out into the fields for lunch. For a baked omelette, pour the mixture into a lightly oiled baking dish and bake at 180°C for 30–40 minutes until golden brown. Cut into wedges if serving as mezza.

12 small marrows (Lebanese zucchini,
    to yield about 750 g pulp)
1 large onion, finely chopped
½ cup roughly chopped flat-leaf parsley
½ cup roughly chopped mint
1 teaspoon salt
½ teaspoon freshly ground black pepper
½ teaspoon ground allspice
½ teaspoon chilli powder (optional)
¾ cup (110 g) self-raising flour, sifted
4 eggs
¾ cup (180 ml) olive oil
mint sprigs and tomato, lettuce and mint
    salad (optional), to serve

Remove the marrow pulp (flesh) using a corer or a small, sharp knife. Squeeze the pulp firmly to remove all moisture, then coarsely chop and place in a bowl. Add the onion, parsley, mint, salt, spices and flour and mix thoroughly. Break in the eggs and mix well.

Heat the oil in a frying pan over high heat. Working in batches, spoon in 1 tablespoon mixture per omelette and lightly pat with a spatula to form a small round. Fry for 3–5 minutes on each side until golden brown, then remove with a slotted spoon to paper towel to drain. Serve hot or cold. The omelettes will keep in a covered container for a couple of days in the refrigerator.

Baked eggplant

Mnazlet batinjan

Serves 6

Eggplant is a Middle Eastern favourite. For this recipe I take care not to overcook it, otherwise the dish becomes too pulpy and uninteresting. You know an eggplant is cooked just right when the outside is soft and has soaked in the flavours of the other ingredients and when the inside is still firm. Be sure to soak the dried split chickpeas the night before you wish to make this recipe.

½ cup (100 g) dried split chickpeas (available from
    Middle Eastern food stores), washed and drained
2 large eggplants, peeled and cut into 1 cm-thick rounds
2½ teaspoons salt
2 tablespoons olive oil
2 onions, thinly sliced
3 large tomatoes, coarsely chopped
½ teaspoon freshly ground black pepper
½ teaspoon ground allspice
2 teaspoons tomato paste
Lebanese rice (see page 158), to serve

Soak the chickpeas with water overnight. Next day, drain.

Preheat the oven to 180°C. Toss the eggplant with ½ teaspoon of the salt and drizzle over 1 tablespoon of the oil. Grill lightly on both sides for 3–4 minutes under a hot griller, then spread in a baking dish.

Heat the remaining oil in a frying pan over high heat and sauté the onion for 4–5 minutes until translucent. Add the chickpeas, tomato, spices, tomato paste, remaining salt and 1½ cups (375 ml) water. Bring to the boil over high heat, then reduce the heat to low and simmer, covered, for 5 minutes. Pour the mixture over the eggplant slices and bake for 20 minutes. Serve with Lebanese rice.

Vegetarian cabbage rolls

Ma'hshi malfouf ateygh

Makes 25-30

Here's another great example of how a traditional Lebanese meat-based dish can be adapted to create a tasty vegetarian version, which is one of the many dishes popular during times of fasting.

1 cabbage, damaged outer leaves discarded
1 head garlic, coarsely chopped
2 large tomatoes, coarsely chopped
juice of 1 lemon, plus extra to serve (optional)

Filling
1½ cups (300 g) basmati or long-grain rice, washed and drained
2 large tomatoes, finely chopped
1 onion, finely chopped
2 cups finely chopped flat-leaf parsley
¼ cup finely chopped mint
¼ cup (60 ml) olive oil
¼ teaspoon ground allspice
¼ teaspoon freshly ground black pepper
½ teaspoon salt, or to taste

Bring a large saucepan of water to the boil. Remove the core of the cabbage, cutting as deeply as possible into it. With the hollow centre down, submerge the cabbage into the boiling water. Remove individual leaves as they soften and break away and place them in a colander to drain.

Set aside a few leaves. Spread the remaining leaves on a chopping board and cut in half lengthways, removing the centre stalk. Cut in half again, trimming to shape the leaves into 8 cm × 11 cm rectangles – don't worry if not all the leaves are evenly sized. Set aside the cabbage trimmings to make the Pan-fried cabbage on page 173.

To make the filling, mix together all the ingredients in a bowl. Take 1 heaped teaspoon of the filling and pile along the top of a quartered cabbage leaf, allowing a little space on both sides, and roll (there is no need to fold in the edges). Squeeze the roll firmly in the palm of your hand to remove any excess water. Repeat until all the filling is used.

Line the base of a medium-sized, heavy-based saucepan with the reserved cabbage leaves. Pack the rolls close together in the pan, but do not press down or pack them too firmly. When a layer is completed, sprinkle with a little garlic and tomato. Repeat until all the rolls are in the pan.

Pour lemon juice over the rolls and add enough water to cover. Cover and bring to the boil over high heat, then reduce the heat to low and cook for 1 hour or until the rice is cooked. Serve hot with a squeeze of lemon juice, if desired.

« Lentils and rice

Mjadra'at addis

Serves 6

It should not surprise anyone that the staples of the Lebanese daily diet make great combinations – lentils and rice is just one of these!

1½ cups (300 g) brown lentils, washed and drained
1½ teaspoons salt
150 ml light olive oil
2 onions, halved and finely sliced
1 cup (200 g) long-grain rice, washed and drained
natural yoghurt and Lebanese garden salad
(see page 51), to serve (optional)

Place the lentils in a saucepan with the salt and 3 cups (750 ml) water. Cover and bring to the boil over high heat. Add another 1 cup (250 ml) of cold water (this prevents the lentils from splitting) and boil for about 15 minutes.

Meanwhile, heat the oil in a frying pan over high heat and cook the onion for 6–7 minutes or until golden brown, stirring regularly to brown evenly. Set aside one-quarter of the onion and add the remainder, together with its oil, to the boiling lentils. Stir in the rice, then add another 1 cup water and cook, covered, over low heat for 20–30 minutes or until the water has been absorbed and the rice is tender.

Spoon the lentil mixture into a shallow bowl or platter and sprinkle the reserved onion over the top. Serve with yoghurt and Lebanese garden salad to the side, if desired.

Spicy potato and onion

Bataata m'tabala

Serves 6

This is a deliciously savoury way of serving up the ubiquitous potato chip. These moreish chips can be served on their own or as an accompaniment to a main dish such as Baked kibbee (see page 105), Kafta on skewers (see page 110) or Lamb on skewers (see page 121).

¼ cup (60 ml) olive oil
3 small onions, halved and cut into 3 mm-thick slices
3 potatoes, quartered and cut into 8 mm-thick slices
½ teaspoon salt
¼ teaspoon freshly ground black pepper
¼ teaspoon ground allspice
pinch of hot chilli powder

Heat the oil in a frying pan over high heat (do not allow the oil to smoke).

Sauté the onion for 4–5 minutes or until translucent, then add the potato, salt and spices and stir. Reduce the heat to medium and cook for about 15 minutes, stirring every few minutes. Serve immediately.

Lebanese 'gnocchi'

Mahkroum bi toum

Serves 6

I remember that as a young girl in Lebanon this was a dish my mother made on days when she was at a loss as to what to give me for lunch. She could always rely on *mahkroum bi toum* because the ingredients were always on hand. Nowadays, I enjoy serving this dish to guests who are only familiar with Italian gnocchi. I love witnessing their dazzled expressions when they first taste it.

2 cups (300 g) plain flour, sifted,
   plus extra for sprinkling
2 teaspoons salt

Sauce
5 cloves garlic, peeled
1 teaspoon salt
½ cup (125 ml) olive oil
2 tablespoons lemon juice
1½ teaspoons dried mint

Combine the flour and 1 teaspoon of the salt in a bowl. Make a well and gradually mix in ¾ cup water to form a dough. Turn out onto a floured surface and knead until well combined and elastic, adding extra flour if the dough sticks.

Sprinkle a little flour on the work surface and roll out the dough to form a 2 cm-wide log. Cut into smaller pieces, about 3 cm × 2 cm. Press your fingers into each piece and roll it up towards you, curling the dough over itself. Set aside. (I also like to run the pieces of dough over the ridged lid of a microwave container, as you can see opposite. The ridges trap the sauce beautifully.)

To make the sauce, mash together the garlic and salt using a mortar and pestle or blend in a food processor. Gradually mix in the oil and lemon juice, one-third at a time, then stir in the mint.

Bring a large saucepan of water to the boil and add the remaining teaspoon of salt. Carefully place the mahkroum in the boiling water and cook for 15 minutes or until soft and doughy. Drain.

Pour the sauce over the top and serve immediately.

Okra in olive oil »

Bamieh bi zayt

Serves 6

Okra is an unusual vegetable that rarely gets much use in cuisines other than Middle Eastern, with the exception, perhaps, of Indian cuisine. This traditional okra dish is strikingly tasty. Okra tends to have a stringy texture when cooked in a casserole, but sautéing it first eliminates the stringiness and also enhances its flavour. To make this a hearty non-vegetarian meal in its own right, add 500 g cubed lean lamb or the same amount of chopped skinless chicken breast or thigh fillets to the cooked onion and garlic and sauté until lightly browned. Continue with the recipe.

olive oil, for cooking
500 g very small okra (about 3 cups)
1 large onion, finely chopped
1 clove garlic, sliced
3 large tomatoes, chopped
2 tablespoons tomato paste
2 teaspoons salt
½ teaspoon freshly ground black pepper
½ teaspoon ground allspice
¼ cup (60 ml) lemon juice
Lebanese rice (see opposite), to serve

Heat 2 tablespoons oil in a frying pan over high heat and fry the okra for 5 minutes or until it just begins to colour. Remove the okra with a slotted spoon and drain on paper towel. Heat a little more oil in the pan and cook the onion and garlic over high heat for 5–6 minutes or until lightly browned. Add the okra, tomato, tomato paste, salt, spices, lemon juice and 3 cups (750 ml) water. Cover and cook for 40 minutes or until the liquid thickens, stirring occasionally. Serve with Lebanese rice.

Lebanese rice »

Riz bi sh'arieh

Serves 6 as an accompaniment

Riz bi sh'arieh is served as an accompaniment to many Lebanese dishes, or can be eaten on its own with yoghurt for a light meal.

50 g butter
1 cup broken egg vermicelli
2 cups (400 g) long-grain rice, washed and drained
1½ teaspoons salt

Melt the butter in a medium-sized saucepan over medium heat, add the vermicelli and cook, stirring, for 3 minutes or until dark golden brown. Stir in the rice, salt and 1 litre water, then cover and bring to the boil over high heat. Reduce the heat to low and cook, covered, for 10–12 minutes or until all the water has been absorbed and the rice is tender. Serve immediately.

« Silverbeet stalks with tahini and lemon juice

Dila' sleeq salak

Serves 6
Suitable for mezza

Use the stalks left over from making the Silverbeet rolls on page 146 in this recipe, which can be served as an entrée or as part of a mezza selection.

3 cups silverbeet stalks, washed and dried,
    ends trimmed
¼ cup (60 ml) lemon juice
¼ cup (70 g) tahini
1 clove garlic, crushed
½ teaspoon salt
flat-leaf parsley leaves, to serve

Chop the silverbeet stalks into bite-sized pieces and place in a small saucepan. Cover with water, cover and bring to the boil. Cook for 10 minutes or until soft. Drain, squeezing out any excess water.

Beat together the lemon juice, tahini, garlic, salt and ¼ cup (60 ml) water. Stir in the silverbeet stalks and toss to coat. Serve hot or at room temperature, scattered with flat-leaf parsley leaves.

Beans with burghul

Mjadra bi loubyeh

Serves 6

This hearty bean and burghul combination is popular during the winter months because it is loaded with protein and fibre. You can vary the consistency of this dish according to your preference by adding more water. Remember to soak the dried beans the night before you wish to cook this recipe.

2 cups (400 g) dried borlotti beans or
    red kidney beans, washed and drained
2 teaspoons salt
1 cup (250 ml) olive oil
4 onions, finely chopped
1½ cups (240 g) coarse burghul (see page 214),
    washed and drained
radishes or natural yoghurt, to serve

Cover the beans with water and soak overnight.

Next day, drain the beans, then cover with fresh water and bring to the boil over medium heat. Reduce the heat to low and simmer, covered, for 90 minutes or until the beans are tender, topping up the water regularly if needed. When the beans are cooked, add the salt.

Heat the oil in a frying pan over high heat and cook the onion for 8–10 minutes or until dark brown, stirring regularly to brown evenly. Drain the oil onto the beans, leaving the onion in the pan. Add 1 cup (250 ml) water to the beans.

Mash the onion with a potato masher, then add 1 cup water and bring to the boil for 2–3 minutes. Add the onion mixture to the beans, then stir in the burghul. Cook, covered, for 30 minutes until the water is absorbed and the burghul is soft. Serve hot or at room temperature with radishes or yoghurt.

Spinach with burghul

Sabanekh bi burghul

Serves 6

Setting aside the fact that burghul is an inexpensive and easy-to-prepare ingredient, the main reason it is always present in some form at every Lebanese meal is because it has an essential energising role in our diet. Spinach with burghul is a desirable combination, yet a mere drop in the ocean as to how we love to use burghul.

2 bunches spinach, washed and drained
100 ml olive oil
1 large onion, chopped
½ cup (80 g) coarse burghul (see page 214),
    washed and drained
½ teaspoon freshly ground black pepper
½ teaspoon freshly ground allspice
1 teaspoon salt
fried thinly sliced onion (optional) to serve

Remove and reserve the spinach stalks and roughly chop the leaves.

Heat the oil in a large saucepan over high heat and sauté the onion for 6–7 minutes or until golden brown. Add the burghul and continue to cook, stirring occasionally, for 5 minutes. Add the spinach leaves and stalks, pepper, allspice and salt and cook for another 3–5 minutes, stirring occasionally, until the spinach has wilted. Serve hot or at room temperature. Garnish with fried thinly sliced onion if desired.

Green beans in olive oil »

Loubyeh bi zayt

Serves 6
Suitable for mezza

I love fresh green beans, as do many Lebanese people, and this is my favourite way to cook them. I often eat this dish on its own, but it is ideal for mezza and excellent as a side dish for chicken served with rice, or served on a bed of Lebanese rice (see page 158) for a strictly vegetarian meal. If you prefer the beans to be crisper, then reduce the cooking time by 10 minutes. This dish can also be made without the tomatoes.

⅔ cup (160 ml) olive oil
2 large onions, chopped
1.5 kg green beans, strings removed
3 large tomatoes, chopped
1½ teaspoons salt (or to taste)
½ teaspoon freshly ground black pepper
½ teaspoon ground allspice

Heat the oil in a saucepan over high heat and sauté the onion for 6–7 minutes or until golden brown. Stir in the beans, then cover and cook for about 5 minutes. Add the tomato, salt and spices, replace the lid and cook over low heat for 30 minutes. Serve hot or at room temperature.

Vegetable stack

Ol'eb khoudra

Serves 6

Here, many of my favourite vegetables are all featured in one attractive dish!

2 large tomatoes, cut into 1 cm-thick rounds
1 large onion, cut into 1 cm-thick rounds
250 g green beans, trimmed
3 carrots, halved widthways, then each half cut
    lengthways into 3 pieces
1 eggplant, peeled and cut into 1 cm-thick slices
1 zucchini, cut into 1 cm-thick slices
250 g pumpkin, peeled, seeded and cut into
    thin wedges
2 potatoes, thinly sliced
180 g small okra (about 1 cup)
1 tablespoon salt
½ teaspoon freshly ground black pepper, plus extra
½ teaspoon ground allspice
1 tablespoon olive oil
tomato slices and flat-leaf parsley leaves, to serve

In a large heavy-based saucepan, make a layer of half the tomato slices, then a layer using all the onion, then alternating layers using all the beans, carrot, eggplant, zucchini, pumpkin, potato and okra. Sprinkle the salt and spices over the top and drizzle with the oil. Finish with a layer of the remaining tomato, then pour over ½ cup (125 ml) water. Cover and bring to the boil over medium heat, then reduce the heat to low and cook for 30 minutes or until the vegetables are tender but still maintain their shape.

Remove the lid from the pan and replace with a large plate or platter. Invert the pan, tipping the layered vegetables onto the plate in one mound. Top with tomato slices and parsley leaves and season with pepper. Serve in large spoonfuls, being sure to ladle some juices over each plate.

Burghul and tomato pilaf

Burghul bi banadoura

Serves 6

The basic idea of most recipes containing burghul is to have it soak in the flavours and juices of the other ingredients. This dish is very tasty and almost a meal in itself. If you prefer a spicier dish, add an extra ½ teaspoon allspice or ¼ teaspoon paprika, or both if you're really game.

2 tablespoons olive oil
2 onions, finely chopped
4 large tomatoes, finely chopped
1 teaspoon salt, or to taste
½ teaspoon ground allspice
½ teaspoon freshly ground black pepper
½ teaspoon hot paprika
2 cups (320 g) coarse burghul (see page 214),
    washed and drained

Heat the oil in a saucepan over high heat and sauté the onion for 6–7 minutes or until golden brown. Add the tomato, salt, allspice, pepper and paprika and cook for 2 minutes.

Stir in the burghul and 2 cups (500 ml) water, then bring to the boil over high heat. Reduce the heat to medium and simmer for 15–20 minutes or until the burghul has softened. Taste the liquid and adjust the seasoning with salt and pepper; add another ½ cup (125 ml) water if the dish is too dry. Cook for another 5 minutes or until all the liquid has been absorbed and the burghul is tender. Serve hot or at room temperature.

Endive in oil »

Hindbe bi zayt

Serves 6

This popular dish combines the peppery and bitter flavour of endive with the sharpness of lemon juice and the sweetness of cooked onion. The flavours are subtle so be careful not to overdo the lemon juice or the spices.

760 g endive (about 2 bunches), ends trimmed,
    stems chopped into 5 cm-lengths and washed
¼ cup (60 ml) light olive oil
2 medium-sized onions, quartered and thinly sliced
¼ teaspoon ground allspice
½ teaspoon salt
¼ teaspoon freshly ground black pepper
⅓ cup (80 ml) lemon juice

Bring a saucepan of water to the boil over high heat, then add the endive and cook for 4 minutes. Drain and set aside to cool.

Meanwhile, heat the oil in a frying pan over medium heat (do not allow the oil to smoke), then add the onion and cook for 6–7 minutes or until golden brown, stirring regularly so the onion cooks evenly.

Remove half of the onion from the pan and set aside. Squeeze out any excess water from the endive, then add the endive to the pan with the remaining onion. Add the allspice, salt and pepper, then stir to combine well and cook for 3–4 minutes for the endive is heated through. Remove from the heat and stir in the lemon juice.

Transfer to a serving plate and spread the reserved onion over the top. Serve hot or at room temperature.

« Lebanese omelette rolls

Ijjie bi laban

Makes 3–4

Lebanese omelettes are almost wafer-like but still moist. When filled with yoghurt and fresh herbs, they make for a light and delicious snack that is always well received by family and friends.

6 eggs
¼ teaspoon ground allspice
¼ teaspoon freshly ground black pepper
½ teaspoon salt
olive oil, for brushing

Filling
1 cup (250 ml) Yoghurt dip (see page 12)
3 spring onions, very finely chopped
⅓ cup finely chopped flat-leaf parsley
⅓ cup finely chopped mint

To make the filling, place the ingredients in a bowl and mix to combine well. Set aside. Break the eggs into a separate bowl, then add the allspice, pepper and salt and gently beat until well combined.

Use a square frying pan if possible. Lightly brush the pan with olive oil and place over medium heat. Pour in ¼–⅓ of the omelette mixture to form a thin layer that covers the whole pan. Do not stir the mixture in the centre or bring it in at the sides as you normally would when making an omelette, and do not turn it over. The omelette should be thin enough to cook all the way through. Gently ease the edges of the omelette off the pan and slide or lift it onto a warm plate. Repeat until all the mixture has been used.

Place one omelette at a time on a clean chopping board. Spread the filling evenly over the surface of each omelette and roll up. Cut each into 3–4 cm pieces, then serve.

White marrow casserole

Yakhanet koussa

Serves 6

The quantity of marrows needed for this recipe will depend on their size. I try to find six that are medium-sized, but if you can only find small ones, select about ten; if the marrows are very large you'll only need two.

6 medium-sized marrows (Lebanese zucchini),
    washed and ends trimmed
2 tablespoons olive oil
3 onions, finely chopped
½ teaspoon ground allspice
½ teaspoon salt
6 cloves garlic, coarsely chopped
½ teaspoon freshly ground black pepper
6 tomatoes, diced
steamed rice, to serve

Slice the marrows in half lengthways, then chop into bite-sized pieces or cubes.

Place a heavy-based flameproof casserole dish over high heat. Add the oil, garlic and onion and cook for 4–5 minutes or until the onion is translucent. Stir in the marrow, allspice, salt and pepper and cook for 1 minute so the marrow takes on the flavours of the garlic and onion. Add the tomato, then reduce the heat to low and cook, covered, for 30 minutes or until the marrow is soft and still succulent. Stir occasionally to prevent sticking.

Serve the casserole on a bed of steamed rice.

PAN-FRIED VEGETABLES

The Lebanese enjoy fried vegetables, which are collectively known as *khoudra maqli*. A dish of fried potato, eggplant and cauliflower is often prepared to accompany fried fish. Pan-fried vegetables are always served with Tahini sauce (see page 19). If you are pan-frying a variety of vegetables, they can be cooked in batches in the same oil.

Pan-fried potato

Bataata maqli

Serves 6

5 potatoes, halved and sliced lengthways into chips
   (or cut into 5 mm-thick rounds)
1 teaspoon salt
2 cups (500 ml) light olive oil
Tahini sauce (see page 19), to serve

Quickly wash and drain the potato pieces and pat dry. Rub the salt into them.

Heat the oil in a deep frying pan over high heat for 2–4 minutes. Add as many potato pieces as you can comfortably fit in the pan and fry for 3–4 minutes on each side. Remove with a slotted spoon and drain on paper towel. Repeat with the remaining potato pieces. Serve immediately with tahini sauce.

Pan-fried eggplant

Batinjan maqli

Serves 6
Suitable for mezza

Soaking the eggplant in salted water before cooking prevents it from absorbing too much oil. However, it will still soak up some of the oil so you may need to use a little extra during cooking.

2 eggplants
1 tablespoon salt
2 cups (500 ml) light olive oil
Tahini sauce (see page 19), to serve

Trim the eggplants and peel roughly (there is no need to peel off all the skin). Cut in half and slice lengthways into 1 cm-thick slices (or cut into 1 cm-thick rounds). Cover completely with cold water, add the salt and leave for 20 minutes. Drain and pat dry with paper towel.

Heat the oil in a deep frying pan over high heat for 2–4 minutes. Add as many eggplant pieces as you can comfortably fit in the pan and fry for 3–4 minutes on each side. Remove with a slotted spoon and drain on paper towel. Repeat with the remaining eggplant pieces. Serve hot or at room temperature with tahini sauce.

Pan-fried cauliflower

Ar'nabit maqli

Serves 6
Suitable for mezza

Cauliflower is too often considered a bland and uninteresting vegetable. Not so for the Lebanese when it is cooked in this way and served with Tahini sauce (see page 19). Soaking the cauliflower pieces in boiling water before cooking softens them a little, which helps them to fry evenly throughout.

1 cauliflower, separated into florets
boiling water, for soaking
¼ teaspoon salt
2 cups (500 ml) light olive oil
Tahini sauce (see page 19), to serve

Slice each floret in half. Place in a bowl, cover with boiling water and leave for 5 minutes. Drain and pat dry with paper towel, then rub in salt to taste.

Heat the oil in a deep frying pan over high heat for 2–4 minutes. Add as many cauliflower pieces as you can comfortably fit in the pan and fry for 5–7 minutes on each side or until golden brown. Remove with a slotted spoon and drain on paper towel. Repeat with the remaining cauliflower pieces. Serve hot or at room temperature with tahini sauce.

Pan-fried cabbage

Makmoura

Serves 6

In traditional Lebanese cooking there is very little wastage – every part of a vegetable is used. For example, you can use the cabbage left over from making Cabbage rolls (see page 132) in this recipe.

100 ml olive oil
1 large onion, finely chopped
½ cabbage, finely chopped
½ cup (80 g) coarse burghul (see page 214),
    washed and drained
½ teaspoon ground allspice
½ teaspoon freshly ground black pepper
1 teaspoon salt

Heat the oil in a large frying pan over high heat and sauté the onion for 6–7 minutes or until golden brown. Add the cabbage, burghul, allspice, pepper and salt and cook over medium heat for 20 minutes or until the cabbage has softened to taste, stirring to avoid sticking. Serve hot or at room temperature.

Laban, or yoghurt, is indispensable to the Lebanese diet. This versatile ingredient is often served with meat dishes and vegetables, but never with fish – it would be a bit like the Italians sprinkling parmesan cheese over their fish-based pasta dishes. When I was growing up in Lebanon, *rowabe* (yoghurt culture) would be kept alive in my mother's kitchen all the time – we couldn't just step out to the corner shop and buy yoghurt the way we can today. I remember being a little surprised to find my uncle Joe making his own laban when I arrived in Melbourne in 1954. He must have preserved the culture to take along with him as I'd seen others do when they readied themselves to migrate to another country. A day or two before boarding the boat, they would take a clean cloth, usually of fine muslin, soak it in someone's freshly made laban, lay it out in a cool place to dry, then carefully wrap it in some clean paper and slip the precious little package into their suitcase.

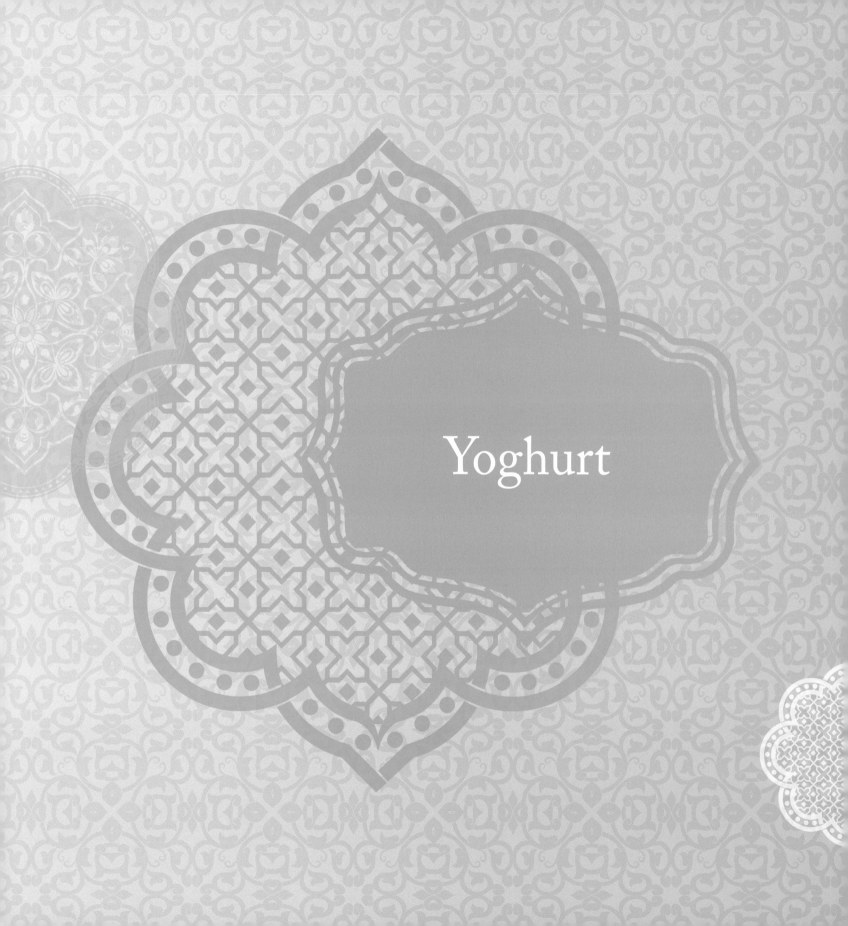

Yoghurt

Homemade yoghurt

Laban

Makes 2 litres

Yoghurt can be made with full-cream or skim milk, the choice is really yours, but full-cream milk does set better.

drop of olive oil
2 litres milk (full-cream or skim)
2 tablespoons natural yoghurt (as culture)

Grease a saucepan with a drop of oil (this makes cleaning the saucepan later much easier because it prevents the milk from sticking). Pour in the milk and bring to the boil over high heat. Remove from the heat, then transfer to a heatproof bowl. Allow to cool slightly until you can dip your little finger in and comfortably leave it there while you count to 12 (the milk should be tepid to warm, and should not burn your finger).

In a small saucer, mix 2 tablespoons of the warm milk with the yoghurt. When well combined, return the mixture to the bowl and stir. Cover with a lid or with plastic film and a plate, then place a heavy blanket on top and set aside in a warm place for 8 hours. Remove the blanket and place the bowl in the refrigerator, where the yoghurt will keep for 2–3 weeks.

Yoghurt balls in olive oil »

Labnee makbous bi zayt

Makes 28 balls
Suitable for mezza

In village homes all over Lebanon, stored among the jars of pickled turnips, olives, stuffed eggplants and an assortment of other vegetables, you will invariably find two or three jars of these appetising yoghurt cheese balls.

2 kg natural yoghurt
salt
olive oil, for rubbing and pouring
hot chillies (optional)
thyme sprigs (optional)

Place the yoghurt in a clean muslin or cheesecloth bag. Tie a knot at the level of the yoghurt and suspend the bag over a bowl. Allow to drain for 2 days.

Line a tray with paper or a tea towel. Remove the yoghurt from the bag and place in a bowl, adding salt to taste. Rub your hands with olive oil (to prevent the yoghurt sticking to your hands) and roll the yoghurt into balls the size of a ping-pong ball. Place on the tray, cover and leave at room temperature for a further 2 days.

Place the yoghurt balls in a sterilised 1.5 litre airtight jar (see page 215), adding the chillies and thyme if desired. Cover with olive oil and refrigerate.

Use within 5–6 weeks as part of a mezza selection, as a snack or on toast for a delicious breakfast.

Yoghurt cheese with chilli and zah'tar

Shankleesh

Makes 4–5 balls
Suitable for mezza

Shankleesh is a specialty of Akkar, a fertile region in the far north of Lebanon. It is a common mezza dish, often accompanied by arak, the aniseed-flavoured favourite Lebanese aperitif, but can also be spread onto Lebanese bread and eaten for breakfast. Making it is a long process, but it is easy and worth the wait.

3 kg natural yoghurt
¼ cup (55 g) salt
2 teaspoons salt, or to taste
½ teaspoon finely ground chilli powder
½ cup zah'tar (see page 215)
olive oil, for brushing
Lebanese bread (see page 24, or purchased)
    and mint sprigs, to serve

Garnish for one shankleesh
1 spring onion, finely chopped
1 tomato, finely diced
1 tablespoon extra virgin olive oil

In a large bowl, mix together the yoghurt, salt and 1 litre water until well combined. Transfer to a large heavy-based saucepan and bring to the boil over high heat and cook for 15–20 minutes. Do not stir at any time. It is essential that the water begins to separate and bubble up, and at this point the yoghurt should resemble ricotta cheese. Remove from the heat and cool to room temperature. Spoon the cheese into a muslin bag and tie or wring the bag tightly at the top. Place the bag in a colander over a bowl to catch the dripping whey. Leave overnight in a cool place.

The next day the cheese should be crumbly but still moist. Discard the whey. Transfer the cheese to a mixing bowl, add the remaining salt and the chilli and work into the cheese until the mixture holds together like a soft dough.

Cover a tray with 2 thick clean tea towels (or several layers of paper towel). Take a generous amount of the cheese mixture and roll it between the palms of your hands to form a ball about the size of a tennis ball. Place on the tray, and repeat with the remaining mixture to make 4–5 balls.

Now begins the drying process. In Lebanon, the cheese balls are normally dried under direct sunlight over a 2-day period, and are brought indoors overnight. However, I recommend keeping the tray indoors. Place the tray by a window that allows sunlight in for most of the day. Change the tea towels or paper towel at the beginning of the second day as they will have absorbed a lot of moisture.

After the second day of drying, transfer the balls to a 1.5 litre-capacity sterilised jar (see page 215), seal and leave for 5–7 days to mature. Like most cheeses, the balls will have formed a covering of mould. This can be gently scraped off with a knife and the ball washed or wiped with a damp cloth.

Spread zah'tar evenly onto a tray. Lightly brush each cheese ball with oil and roll in zah'tar until evenly coated. Store in an airtight container in the refrigerator for up to 3 months.

To serve, combine the garnish ingredients. Mash 1 shankleesh with the mixture and serve with Lebanese bread and mint.

Lebanese 'tortellini' in yoghurt

Sheish barak

Serves 6

This is a truly warming and hearty dish to eat in cold weather, although for the Lebanese it is a year-round favourite. The meat-filled parcels resemble Italian tortellini, but what sets this dish apart is the rich yoghurt sauce flavoured with garlic and mint.

2 cups (300 g) plain flour, sifted
½ teaspoon salt
mint leaves, to garnish

Filling
1 teaspoon butter
1 onion, chopped
375 g coarsely minced lean lamb
2 teaspoons salt
¼ teaspoon freshly ground black pepper
¼ teaspoon ground allspice

Yoghurt sauce
1 kg natural yoghurt
1 tablespoon plain flour, sifted
½ cup (100 g) long-grain rice,
   washed and drained
1 teaspoon salt
1 egg
1 litre boiling water
3 large cloves garlic, peeled
½ teaspoon salt
20 g butter
1 teaspoon dried mint

To make the filling, melt the butter in a frying pan over high heat and cook the onion for 4–5 minutes or until translucent. Add the meat and fry for 5 minutes, then stir in the salt, pepper and allspice and cook for another 5 minutes. Set aside.

Combine the flour and salt, then add ¾ cup (180 ml) water and mix to form a dough. Turn out onto a floured surface and knead well. Roll out the dough to a thickness of 3 mm and cut into 4 cm rounds. Flatten each round with your fingers and place 1 teaspoon filling in the centre. Fold over to create a half-moon shape and pinch the edges together to seal. Pull the ends down, then fold them over and press together. The dumplings should resemble little bowler hats.

To make the sauce, combine the yoghurt, flour, rice, salt and egg in a large saucepan and bring to the boil over high heat, stirring constantly. Add the boiling water, then reduce the heat to low and simmer, stirring constantly, for about 30 minutes or until the rice is cooked.

Carefully add the dumplings to the pan of sauce. Increase the heat to high and stir a couple of times (do not cover the pan or the yoghurt will curdle).

Crush the garlic with the salt using a mortar and pestle. Melt the butter in a small saucepan over high heat and cook the garlic for 2 minutes until slightly brown. Add to the yoghurt sauce with the dried mint and cook gently over low heat for 10–15 minutes. Garnish the dumplings with mint leaves and serve immediately.

Chickpeas with yoghurt

Fattet hummus bi laban

Serves 6

Fattet is the generic name for a dish that combines layers of crispy pieces of Lebanese bread with a vegetable or grain, regardless of whether the recipe calls for meat or not. This one doesn't, but I know of a version that includes minced lamb and is equally as popular throughout Lebanon and other parts of the Middle East. Remember to soak the dried chickpeas the night before you wish to make this.

1 cup (200 g) dried chickpeas, washed and drained
    or 2 cups drained tinned chickpeas
pinch of bicarbonate of soda
½ teaspoon salt, plus a pinch extra
80 g butter
½ cup (80 g) pine nuts
1 round of Lebanese bread (see page 24,
    or use purchased), split in half widthways
    and cut into 2 cm squares
1 clove garlic, crushed
1 cup (280 g) natural yoghurt

If using dried chickpeas, cover the chickpeas with water, add the bicarbonate of soda and soak overnight.

Next day, drain the chickpeas and place in a saucepan. Cover with fresh water, add the salt and bring to the boil. Reduce the heat to low and simmer, covered, for about 30 minutes. Set aside.

Meanwhile, melt 60 g of the butter in a frying pan over medium heat and cook the bread pieces in batches, stirring to ensure they brown evenly. Keep an eye on the heat to make sure the butter does not burn. Drain on paper towel.

Melt the remaining butter in the same pan over medium heat and cook the pine nuts for 2–3 minutes or until golden, stirring constantly to prevent them from burning. Drain on paper towel. Stir the garlic and remaining pinch of salt into the yoghurt and whisk until smooth.

Drain the chickpeas, reserving ¼ cup (60 ml) of the cooking liquid. Stir the reserved liquid into half of the drained chickpeas and make a rough purée by mashing with a wooden spoon or blending in a food processor on low speed for no more than 1 minute. Fold in the remaining chickpeas.

To serve, arrange two-thirds of the fried bread evenly on a platter or 6 plates, then spread the chickpea purée over the top, followed by the yoghurt. Top with the remaining bread and finish with a sprinkling of pine nuts.

Eat immediately as the bread will quickly become soggy if left for too long.

Lebanese sweets are not necessarily served as, nor are they considered to be, desserts. A Lebanese 'dessert' traditionally consists of a large platter of fresh seasonal fruit. Sweets are usually served with coffee at the very end of a meal. Most Lebanese sweets are affiliated with a religious celebration, or are made to herald a special family occasion. For example, doughnuts (see page 201) are made to celebrate the baptism of Christ and the ma'amoul (see page 193) are for Easter. There is a variation on the Rice pudding (see page 208), called *meghli*, which is prepared to mark the birth of a baby.

Whatever the occasion, sweets are an essential part of Lebanese hospitality. They are always on offer, with coffee, when a visitor comes. An Australian friend, Anne, shared many a time with me in my kitchen. I would cook and share recipes for Lebanese sweets and in exchange Anne would help me gratify my children's acquired cravings for fairy cakes and cupcakes.

Sweets & Drinks

Sugar syrup

Attir

Makes about 250 ml

Sugar syrup is required in several of the recipes that follow, and can be made so that it has either a thick or thin consistency. The thin syrup is ideal for Doughnuts (see page 201) and Sweet dumplings (see page 202), while the thick syrup is good for Walnut-filled pancakes (see page 206), Baklava (page 202) and Sweet cheese (page 211). Sugar syrup can be used hot or cold; the general rules are 'hot on hot' (that is, use hot or warm syrup on a hot or warm dish) and 'cold on cold' (likewise). This allows the syrup to soak well into the sweet (a tip given to me by a sweet-maker in Tripoli). The lemon juice in the recipes prevents the sugar forming lumps as it boils.

Thin sugar syrup

Attir

400 g white sugar
1 tablespoon lemon juice
1 tablespoon rosewater (see page 215)

Bring the sugar and 2 cups (500 ml) water slowly to the boil in a saucepan over low heat. Add the lemon juice and continue boiling over low heat for 10–15 minutes until the syrup is the consistency of honey. Stir in the rosewater and remove from the heat. Depending on the recipe, use while still hot or allow to cool and store in the refrigerator for up to 2 weeks.

Thick sugar syrup

Attir

800 g white sugar
1 tablespoon lemon juice
1 tablespoon rosewater (see page 215)

Bring the sugar, lemon juice and 2½ cups (625 ml) water to the boil over medium heat. Cover and boil for 20 minutes until the sugar has completely dissolved and the syrup is thick. Stir in the rosewater and remove from the heat. Depending on the recipe, use while still hot or allow to cool and store in the refrigerator for up to 2 weeks.

Lebanese cream

Ashta

Makes about 700 ml

Ashta is used as a filling or topping in Lebanese desserts. It can be served with Sweet cheese with syrup (see page 211) and as a filling for Sweet ladies' fingers (page 201) or Walnut-filled pancakes (page 206).

2 litres full-cream milk
2 cups (500 ml) pouring cream

Mix the milk and cream together in a jug and pour into a heavy-based saucepan. Bring to the boil over high heat, then reduce the heat to low and simmer gently for 1–1½ hours. Skim the froth from the top and place in a bowl. Continue to skim the froth until there is no mixture left. Cool to room temperature, then chill in the refrigerator for 2–3 days.

Tahini syrup

Dibis bi tahini

Makes about 250 ml

This delicious sweet snack is commonly eaten spread over Lebanese bread (see page 24) like honey.

1 cup carob molasses (see page 214)
¼ cup (70 g) tahini

Mix together the molasses and tahini. Store in a covered container for up to 1 week. (Dibis does not need to be refrigerated as long as it is covered.)

Easter sweets

Ma'amoul

Makes about 30

Many years ago, about a week before Easter, a bishop from Lebanon visited Melbourne and was doing the rounds of the Lebanese community. Lebanese hospitality being what it is, naturally at every household he was greeted with a cup of coffee. By the time he reached my front door he'd had enough, and before I had the chance to offer a cup, he begged, 'Please, no coffee!' But my daughter, who had just brewed some, interceded, saying, 'Are you sure? *Ma'mool!*' Now, in the region of Lebanon where I come from, *ma'mool* means 'It's made' or 'It's ready'. The bishop misunderstood and thought she was referring to the Easter sweet, ma'amoul, so he replied, 'Oh yes, I'll have one of those.' You can't imagine the thoughts that went through my head – Easter was another week away, and to have Easter cakes already prepared in anticipation of the celebrations was the furthest thing from my mind!

To make authentic ma'amoul you will need to source a ma'amoul mould (see page 190) from a Middle Eastern grocer. For a change, try using the date filling from Date biscuits (see page 198).

3 cups (480 g) fine semolina (see page 215)
250 g unsalted butter, softened
½ teaspoon white sugar
1 teaspoon mahlab (optional, see page 215)
1 teaspoon dried yeast
2 tablespoons orange-blossom water (see page 215)
¼ cup (60 ml) milk
icing sugar, for sprinkling (optional)

Filling
1 cup (120 g) coarsely chopped pistachio nuts or walnuts
¼ cup (55 g) white sugar
1 tablespoon orange-blossom water (see page 215)

Place the semolina, butter and sugar in a bowl and rub together with your fingertips. Leave to rest for 1 hour covered with plastic film. Add the mahlab (if using), yeast, orange-blossom water and milk and mix together to form a dough. Turn out onto a work surface, then knead. Return to the bowl, cover and leave to sit for another 30 minutes.

Preheat the oven to 220°C.

Knead the dough for 5 minutes to help bind it together.

To make the filling, combine all the ingredients. Spoon 1 tablespoon semolina dough into your hand and shape into a ball. Make a hole in the centre and fill with 1 teaspoon of the filling. Seal firmly and flatten slightly in the palm of your hand. Press the dough firmly into a ma'amoul mould, then tap out. Continue with the remaining dough and filling.

Place the ma'amoul about 2.5 cm apart on ungreased baking trays and bake for 15 minutes or until golden. Transfer to wire racks to cool. Sprinkle the biscuits with icing sugar (if using) and store in an airtight container for up to 2 weeks.

Sesame biscuits

Barrosi

Makes about 30

Barrosi are always popular, especially when homemade, and are ideal for when you're feeling peckish. They are light, so having one or two in between meals will not spoil your appetite.

¾ cup (165 g) white sugar
250 g unsalted butter, softened
¼ cup (60 ml) sunflower oil
3 cups (450 g) self-raising flour, sifted
¾ cup (180 ml) milk
1 teaspoon ground aniseed
3 teaspoons mahlab (optional, see page 215)
plain flour, for dusting

Sesame topping
1 cup (150 g) sesame seeds
1½ teaspoons white sugar
¼ cup (60 ml) milk

Preheat the oven to 180°C. Lightly grease a baking tray.

To make the topping, dry-roast the sesame seeds in a frying pan over medium heat for 2–3 minutes, stirring constantly to prevent burning. Remove when golden and fragrant and leave to cool. Once cooled, combine in a shallow bowl with the sugar and milk.

In a large bowl, mix together the sugar, butter and oil. Add the flour, milk, aniseed and mahlab (if using) and mix to make a soft dough. Divide the dough into thirds.

Roll out one-third of the dough on a lightly floured surface to a thickness of 5 mm. Cut into rounds using a 7 cm cutter and press one side of each round in the sesame topping. Place the biscuits, topping-side up, 3 cm apart on a lightly greased baking tray, and bake for 10–12 minutes or until golden. Cool on a wire rack.

Repeat with the remaining dough and sesame topping (there is no need to grease the baking tray again).

Store the biscuits in an airtight container for up to 4 weeks.

Lebanese shortbread

Ghraybi

Makes about 30

Here is a sweet with integrity – short on ingredients but big on taste, Lebanese shortbread is irresistible.

1 cup (160 g) icing sugar
250 g unsalted butter, softened
2½ cups (225 g) plain flour, sifted
about 30 pine nuts

Preheat the oven to 200°C.

Place the icing sugar in a bowl and rub in the butter until the mixture is creamy. Gradually add the flour, rubbing with your fingertips until the mixture achieves a soft consistency and does not stick to your hands.

Shape 1 teaspoon of the mixture into a 6 cm-long oval shape and press one pine nut in the centre. Continue until all the mixture and pine nuts are used.

Place the biscuits about 2.5 cm apart on ungreased baking trays and bake for 12–15 minutes or until lightly browned. Transfer to a wire rack to cool. Store the biscuits in an airtight container for up to 4 weeks.

Orange biscuits

Kaak

Makes about 60

These twice-baked crisp biscuits are made with mahlab, a spice made from the St Lucie cherry that is widely used throughout the Middle East as a flavouring. Sachets of mahlab can usually be found at Middle Eastern food stores.

⅓ cup (75 g) white sugar
1 cup (250 ml) light olive oil
1 cup (250 ml) orange juice
½ teaspoon freshly grated nutmeg
½ teaspoon ground aniseed
2 tablespoons mahlab (see page 215)
5 cups (750 g) self-raising flour
2 teaspoons sesame seeds

Preheat the oven to 250°C and line 2 baking trays with baking paper.

Combine the sugar, oil, orange juice, nutmeg, aniseed and mahlab in a large bowl. Gradually add the flour and work the ingredients into a soft dough. Divide the dough into quarters. Roll each quarter into a 7–8 cm-wide log the same length as a baking tray and place 2 logs on each tray. Cut each log into 1–2 cm-thick sections. Sprinkle the sesame seeds evenly over the logs and lightly pat the seeds into the dough. Bake for 20–25 minutes. Remove from the oven and cool to room temperature. (I turn the oven off, then reheat it to 220°C for the second baking.)

When cooled, separate each biscuit with a knife and place them on the baking trays. Return to the oven and bake for another 15–20 minutes until crisp and golden. Transfer to a wire rack to cool. Store the biscuits in an airtight container for up to 4 weeks.

Date biscuits

Kark bi tamar

Makes about 30

Because they are known to be vitamin-rich, dates are considered important to the Lebanese diet. Even when making sweets, the Lebanese have one eye on flavour and the other on nutrition.

125 g butter, softened
1 tablespoon sunflower oil
¼ cup (55 g) white sugar
2 cups (300 g) self-raising flour, sifted
2 teaspoons mahlab (optional, see page 215)
1 teaspoon ground aniseed
½ (125 ml) cup milk
500 g dried dates, pitted and minced

Topping
½ cup (75 g) sesame seeds
1 teaspoon white sugar
¼ cup (60 ml) milk

Preheat the oven to 180°C and grease a baking tray.

Put the butter, oil and sugar in a large bowl. Add the flour, mahlab (if using), aniseed and milk and mix thoroughly.

Place the dates and 2 tablespoons water in a saucepan over low heat and stir for about 5 minutes until softened to a paste. Cool.

To make the topping, dry-roast the sesame seeds for 2–3 minutes in a frying pan over medium heat, stirring constantly to prevent burning. Remove when golden and fragrant and allow to cool. Once cooled, combine with the other topping ingredients in a shallow bowl.

Spread about half of the topping on a large strip (about 40 cm) of baking paper. Spread a quarter of the biscuit mixture over the topping and, using your hands, fold into a 35 cm × 10 cm flat log. Spread a quarter of the date filling down the centre. Bring the ends together and seal the edges, smoothing and pressing firmly to make a roll (roll the log over the bench to round it, if need be). Repeat with the remaining mixture to make four rolls, adding more topping to the paper as needed. Cut the rolls on the diagonal into 2–3 cm-thick pieces.

Place on the greased baking tray 3 cm apart and bake for 15 minutes until golden. You may need to do this in batches. Transfer to wire racks to cool.

Store the biscuits in an airtight container for up to 4 weeks.

Semolina slice

Nummoora

Makes about 50

Many traditional Lebanese sweets are made with semolina. Of these, *nummoora* is perhaps the most famous throughout the Middle East.

800 g coarsely ground semolina (see page 215)
2 teaspoons baking powder
1 cup (220 g) white sugar
250 g unsalted butter, melted and cooled slightly
1 cup (250 ml) milk
2 tablespoons tahini
about 50 blanched almonds, halved
1 quantity Thin sugar syrup (see page 188), hot

Place the semolina, baking powder and sugar in a bowl. Pour the butter over and mix to combine, then stir in the milk. Cover a 24 cm × 36 cm baking tray with a lip evenly with tahini. Pour the semolina mixture into the tray, smooth out the surface and leave to sit for 1 hour.

Preheat the oven to 230°C.

Slice the semolina on the diagonal into 3.5 cm × 5 cm diamond shapes, then place one split almond in the centre of each diamond. Bake for 50 minutes, then remove from the oven and pour the hot syrup evenly over the top. Cool and serve.

Store the slice in an airtight container for up to 1 week.

Date slice

Lafet el balah

Makes about 20

Here is another dessert dish in which the emphasis is as much on sweetness as it is on nutrition, hence the abundance of essential ingredients such as dates and nuts.

250 g dried dates, pitted and minced
1½ cups coarsely crushed plain sweet biscuits
½ cup (50 g) coarsely crushed walnuts or pistachio nuts
1 cup (90 g) desiccated coconut

Combine the dates and 2 tablespoons water in a saucepan over low heat and stir for 5 minutes or until softened to a paste. Add the biscuit pieces and nuts and cook, stirring, for about 10 minutes.

Sprinkle ½ cup (45 g) of the desiccated coconut on a work surface and place half of the date mixture on top. Using your hands, roll until the coconut has been absorbed. Wrap in foil. Repeat with the remaining coconut and date mixture. Freeze for 1 hour.

Cut the rolls into thin slices on the diagonal to serve. Store in an airtight container for up to 1 week.

« Doughnuts

Awwamaat

Makes about 20

These doughnuts are prepared in huge quantities on 25 September every year to celebrate the martyrdom of Saint Moura, who was crucified for refusing to give up her faith. Every year on that feast day, a friend of mine would visit with a tray laden with these small, light doughnuts. Her name was Moura and my family would go mad for her doughnuts.

2 cups (150 g) self-raising flour, sifted
1 teaspoon dried yeast
1 tablespoon white sugar
1⅓ cups (330 ml) warm water
1 quantity Thin sugar syrup (see page 188), warmed
canola oil or light olive oil, for deep-frying

Place the flour, yeast, sugar and water in a bowl and mix together well. Cover with a heavy cloth (even a blanket) and set aside for 2 hours.

Place the hot syrup in a bowl next to the stove. Heat the oil to very hot, then reduce the heat to medium. Working in batches, carefully drop in tablespoonfuls of doughnut mixture, a few at a time – they will quickly rise to the surface and turn golden. Carefully lift out with a slotted spoon and place in the syrup for a couple of minutes so the doughnuts absorb the syrup.

Remove the doughnuts and place on a platter. Serve hot or at room temperature. These doughnuts are best eaten on the day of making.

Sweet ladies' fingers

Zund el sit

Makes 16–18

The Lebanese are more inclined to have fruit rather than a sweet dish for dessert. However, there are some sweets that should not be passed over – *zund el sit* is one of them.

1 × 375 g packet filo pastry
1 quantity Lebanese cream (see page 189) or 375 g fresh ricotta cheese mixed with 2 tablespoons white sugar and 2 tablespoons rosewater (see page 215)
canola oil or light olive oil, for deep-frying
1 quantity Thick sugar syrup (see page 188), warmed
¼ cup (35 g) crushed pistachio nuts (optional)

Remove the filo pastry from its packaging but do not unroll. Measure and cut two 8 cm lengths from the roll (return the remaining pastry to its packaging and store in the refrigerator for another use). Cut each of these lengths in half along the fold in the pastry roll. Unroll a cut portion of pastry, then take 3 strips and place them on top of each other vertically, then place another 3 strips on top of each other horizontally at the base of the pastry strip to form an upside-down 'T'. Place 1 tablespoon of the cream in the centre of the horizontal strip, where the 'T' joins. Bring in the sides and fold over to enclose the cream, then roll along the vertical pastry strip to form a neat cylindrical parcel. Repeat this process until all pastry and cream are used.

Heat the oil in a frying pan over high heat until really hot, then reduce the heat to medium. Deep-fry the pastries until golden on all sides – this will only take a few minutes and you will need to turn them. Carefully lift from the pan with a slotted spoon and drain on paper towel.

Place the pastries on a platter and pour the warmed syrup over the top. Sprinkle with crushed pistachios, if desired.

Baklava »

Baklawa

Makes about 25 pieces

Baklava can be found throughout the Mediterranean and Middle East. The recipes only vary in the type of nuts used and in the presentation. It can be made in the shape of a cigar, a floret or a diamond. The key to a good baklava is finding the right balance of sweetness between the sweet itself and the syrup. One of my 'aunties', Mrs Deab, taught me how to make baklava. Nowadays we can buy filo pastry, but Mrs Deab would make her own, rolling it out paper-thin.

1 × 375 g packet filo pastry
250 g unsalted butter, melted
2 cups (260 g) finely ground cashews
½ quantity Thick sugar syrup (see page 188), hot
¼ cup (30 g) coarsely ground pistachio nuts (optional)

Preheat the oven to 220°C. Cut the filo pastry sheets to the size of your baking tin; a good size is 25 cm × 35 cm. Brush the baking tin liberally with melted butter. Layer half the filo pastry sheets in the tin, brushing every second sheet with butter. Spread the cashews evenly over the pastry. Cover with the remaining filo, brushing every second sheet with butter. Do not butter the top layer.

With a sharp knife, make parallel cuts on the diagonal about 3.5 cm apart through to the base of the tin, then cut on the diagonal the other way to create diamond shapes. Brush the remaining butter on top.

Bake for 10 minutes, then reduce the temperature to 180°C and bake for another 35 minutes or until golden. Remove from the oven. Pour the hot syrup over the hot pastry. Sprinkle with pistachio nuts (if using) and leave to cool. Store in an airtight container for up to 2 weeks.

Sweet dumplings »

Mahkroum bi succar

Makes about 20

Mahkroum is Lebanese for macaroni or gnocchi. It might appear a little strange to be using a pasta-like dough for a sweet, but it's a standard feature of desserts across the Middle East and many Asian countries, as well as in Europe. I believe the Middle Eastern traders of old introduced pasta dough as a sweet to Sicily. There they have a similar dish using orange-blossom honey instead of sugar syrup.

3 cups (450 g) plain flour, sifted, plus extra for dusting
1 teaspoon ground aniseed
1 tablespoon white sugar
¾ cup (180 ml) vegetable oil
1 quantity Thin sugar syrup (see page 188), warmed
1 cup (250 ml) light olive oil

Place the flour, aniseed, sugar and vegetable oil in a bowl and mix with fingertips. Add 1 cup (250 ml) water and mix together to form a dough. Turn out onto a floured surface, then knead until smooth. Roll out the dough into a rectangle on a lightly floured surface. Cut into 11 cm × 2 cm pieces. Roll out each piece and cut into 3 cm × 2 cm rectangles. Press your fingers into each piece and roll it up towards you, curling the dough over itself. (Lightly press each dumpling onto a sieve or colander if you wish to create a criss-cross pattern). Set aside.

Place the warm syrup in a bowl next to the stove. Heat the oil in a saucepan over high heat until hot, then, working in batches, add the dumplings and cook for 2–3 minutes or until golden. Lift out with a slotted spoon and place in the syrup for a couple of minutes so the dumplings absorb the syrup. Remove and place on a platter. Serve hot or cold. The dumplings are best eaten immediately, but will keep, covered, at room temperature for 24 hours.

Cream caramel

Crème caramel

Serves 8

Many of you will be wondering why I have included cream caramel in a Lebanese cookbook, for this dessert is certainly not of Lebanese origin. But Lebanon was under the French mandate from 1920 through to 1943, a time when Beirut was considered 'the Paris of the Middle East'. Lebanon inherited a range of French culinary influences during that time, the most popular being cream caramel.

My recipe in no way differs from the classic French one, but I include it here because for me it is a sweet aftertaste of Lebanon's past – and therefore my past – when the Lebanese people declared their independence. In remembrance, I prepare this dish each year on 22 November, the day that the independence of Lebanon was internationally recognised in 1943. This dessert needs to be cooked the day before you plan to eat it.

2 litres milk
9 eggs
1 tablespoon whisky
1 tablespoon vanilla sugar (available at most supermarkets)
2 cups (440 g) white sugar

Bring the milk slowly to the boil in a large saucepan over low heat, then remove from the heat and allow to cool.

Preheat the oven to 200°C.

In a large bowl, beat the eggs, whisky, vanilla sugar and 1 cup (220 g) of the sugar with hand-held electric beaters for 2 minutes. Add the cooled milk and beat for 30 seconds.

Place the remaining sugar in a round 25 cm wide × 10 cm deep flameproof dish. To caramelise the sugar, place over medium heat until the sugar has dissolved completely and is golden. Remove from the heat.

Tilt the dish to spread the syrup around the sides, then pour in the milk and egg mixture. Place the dish in a larger roasting tin or baking dish. Add boiling water to come quarter way up sides of dish. Bake for 30 minutes, then reduce the temperature to 180°C and cook for another 45 minutes. Test the cream caramel the same way you would test a cake, by inserting a skewer or cake tester in the centre – it should come out clean. Remove from the oven and loosen the cream caramel from the side of dish with a knife. Cool and refrigerate overnight.

When ready to serve, carefully turn out onto a large, shallow platter with a lip to catch the caramel. Serve at room temperature cut into wedges.

Walnut-filled pancakes

Atoyif

Makes 20

These spongy little pancakes are heavenly and are a typical Lebanese Christmas sweet. After a particularly heavy Christmas lunch, serve them quite some time after the meal with coffee or fresh fruit. For a different filling, try using Lebanese cream (see page 189).

½ cup (80 g) coarsely ground semolina (see page 215)
3 cups (450 g) self-raising flour, sifted
1 tablespoon white sugar
1 cup (250 ml) milk
3 cups (750 ml) warm water
butter, for pan-frying
¼ cup (30 g) coarsely ground pistachio nuts (optional)
1 quantity Thick sugar syrup (see page 188)

Filling
2 cups (280 g) finely crushed walnuts
½ cup (110 g) white or soft brown sugar
2 tablespoons rosewater (see page 215)

Place the semolina, flour, sugar, milk and water in a large bowl and mix together by hand, then mix with hand-held electric beaters until the batter is smooth.

To make the filling, combine the ingredients in a separate bowl.

Melt a little butter in a small non-stick frying pan over medium heat. Working in batches, pour in ¼ cup (60 ml) batter and cook for 1–2 minutes or until the mixture bubbles and dries. Do not turn. Remove and place cooked-side down on a wire rack or tea towel. Repeat with the remaining batter. As you go, cool the pancakes for 1–2 minutes, then stack in pairs with the bubble-sides facing each other.

Place 1 tablespoon of the filling in the centre of each pancake, on the bubble side. Fold the pancake over, bringing the edges together and pressing firmly so that they stick.

To serve, sprinkle with crushed pistachio nuts, if desired, and pour the syrup over.

Rice pudding

Riz bi haleeb

Serves 6–8

Rice pudding is typically associated with English cuisine, but I don't think this recipe has anything to do with the presence of the British in Lebanon in 1941. Rice, after all, is a staple ingredient in the Lebanese diet. The main differences between Lebanese and British rice puddings are the flavouring and the manner of cooking. The British flavour their version with vanilla and sometimes finish off the pudding by baking it in a low oven, whereas the Lebanese simmer the rice on the stovetop until cooked all the way through and flavour it with rosewater.

1 cup (50 g) short-grain rice, washed and drained
1 litre milk
1 cup (220 g) white sugar
2 tablespoons rosewater (see page 215)
1 tablespoon pistachio nuts, crushed

Place the rice in a heavy-based saucepan with 2 cups (500 ml) water and bring to the boil. Reduce the heat to low and cook slowly for about 20 minutes, stirring regularly. Taste to see if the rice is cooked – if necessary add another ½ cup (125 ml) water and continue to cook until the water has been absorbed. When ready, the rice will be fluffy and soft.

Stir in the milk and sugar and cook for 30 minutes, stirring regularly, until thick and creamy. Stir in the rosewater about 5 minutes before the end. Serve hot, warm or cold in a large bowl or individual serving dishes, sprinkled with crushed pistachio nuts.

Fig conserve »

M'rabba al teen

Makes 2 × 500 ml-capacity jars

M'rabba al teen is more like an Eastern European-style candied fruit than a traditional English-style fruit conserve or jam. It can be eaten for breakfast, spread onto Lebanese bread, served with coffee and walnuts, or used to accompany a cheese platter.

⅓ cup (80 ml) olive oil
1½ cups (105 g) blanched almonds, split in half
250 g white sugar
1 teaspoon whole aniseeds (see page 214), washed
juice of 1 lemon
1 kg dried figs, tough stems removed
**   and discarded, thinly sliced**

Heat the oil in a small saucepan over medium heat and cook the almonds for 2–3 minutes or until golden brown, stirring constantly to prevent burning. Remove with a slotted spoon and drain on paper towel. (Alternatively, line a baking tray with baking paper, spread the almonds on top in an even layer and dry-roast in a 220°C oven for 3–4 minutes.)

Place the sugar and 1 cup (250 ml) water in a saucepan and bring to the boil over high heat. When the sugar has dissolved, stir in the aniseeds and lemon juice and boil for another 2–3 minutes. Add the figs and almonds, reduce the heat to low and cook for 20–30 minutes or until all the water has been absorbed and the mixture has thickened. Stir regularly to combine the ingredients well and stop the mixture sticking to the pan. Remove from the heat and cool to room temperature.

Spoon into 2 sterilised 500 ml-capacity airtight jars (see page 215) and seal until ready to use. This conserve can be eaten immediately and doesn't need to be refrigerated.

« Sweet cheese with syrup

Halawat el jibeen

Serves 6–10

Akkawi is the traditional Lebanese cheese used for making this dish. It can be found in Middle Eastern grocery stores. If you can't find it, fresh mozzarella makes a good substitute.

1½ cups (375 ml) water
½ cup (110 g) white sugar
500 g unsalted akkawi cheese (see page 214) or
    fresh mozzarella, cut into small pieces
1 cup (160 g) fine semolina (see page 215)
1 quantity Thick sugar syrup (see page 188), warmed
1 cup (250 ml) Lebanese cream (see page 189)
1 tablespoon pistachio nuts, crushed

Bring the water to the boil in a large saucepan over high heat. Add the sugar and stir for 4 minutes or until dissolved. Add the cheese, stirring continuously for 8–10 minutes or until it has melted and the mixture is smooth. Slowly add the semolina in a thin, steady stream, stirring continuously for another 5 minutes or until well combined. The mixture will be smooth and thick. Remove the pan from the heat.

Pour the warmed sugar syrup onto a large, clean non-stick surface. Add the hot cheese mixture and quickly roll out using a rolling pin. Very quickly pull and stretch the mixture by hand, breaking off the stretched pieces. Arrange the pieces on a large platter, cover with plastic film and then place in the refrigerator to chill.

When ready to serve, spoon the Lebanese cream over the cheese and sprinkle with crushed pistachio nuts. Divide among dessert plates and eat with a fork.

Rosewater lemonade

Lemonada

Makes about 1 litre

I always keep homemade lemonade at the restaurant as an alternative to carbonated drinks. The nice thing about making your own lemonade is that you get a full lemon taste, and you can be sure there are no additives. Fresh lemonade is especially fantastic in the sweltering summer heat.

5 tablespoons white sugar
1 litre cold water
1 cup (250 ml) lemon juice
1 tablespoon rosewater (see page 215)

Add the sugar to the water and stir until the sugar has dissolved. Stir in the lemon juice and rosewater. Serve immediately or chill for later. Store in a jug in the refrigerator for up to 5 days.

Lebanese Coffee

Ahawe

Serves 8

Coffee is very much a part of the Lebanese tradition of generosity and hospitality. Anyone who comes into the home is offered a cup of coffee, whatever the time of day. Lebanese coffee is brewed in a pot known as a *raqwi*. There are two types of raqwi: one for brewing the coffee and the other for serving it. The pot used for brewing is open-topped, made of brass or enamel and has a long handle. The coffee is added to boiling water in the pot, then stirred and brought back to the boil. The coffee is then transferred to a more ornate-looking raqwi with a lid to serve. The coffee is covered with the lid to keep it hot, and then it is left for a few moments to allow the sediment to settle before pouring the coffee into small cups called *chaffette* (see opposite). Both types of raqwi are not difficult to obtain nowadays as they are readily available from Middle Eastern grocery stores or suppliers.

Lebanese coffee does not refer to a particular variety of coffee bean or to a special blend. As with Turkish coffee, it refers to the type of grind, which is very fine, almost pulverised. To achieve the rich, full-flavoured coffee that is the hallmark of Lebanese hospitality, I suggest you try a blend of coffee beans from Ethiopia, Colombia and Papua New Guinea. And I recommend you use Arabica-quality coffee because it is more flavoursome than Robusta, which is primarily used for producing instant coffee. A sense of ceremony is perhaps the only distinguishing feature between Lebanese and Turkish coffee.

The serving of coffee is embedded in ceremony. Often the host or hostess will personally hand around the tray of poured shot coffees. Older people are held in very high esteem and are offered coffee first as a mark of respect.

2 cardamom pods, split (optional)
1 tablespoon white sugar
2 tablespoons ground coffee

Place 2 cups (500 ml) water and the cardamom (if using) in a medium-sized raqwi and bring to the boil. Add the sugar and then the coffee. Hold the raqwi a little above the stove over medium heat so that the coffee boils, but does not boil over. Do not sit the raqwi directly on the heat. While the coffee is boiling, stir only the top, then keep stirring until the froth disappears. Remove from the heat.

Cover the raqwi with a saucer or lid and leave to sit for a few minutes so the sediment settles to the bottom. Serve.

Glossary

Akkawi
The Arabic name for a white unsalted cheese traditionally made from sheep's or goat's milk. It is the cheese used in Sweet Cheese with Syrup (see page 211) and can be bought from Middle Eastern grocery stores. Mozzarella cheese makes a good substitute.

Allspice
Also known as pimento, allspice is a member of the myrtle family and tastes like a combination of cloves, cinnamon and nutmeg. It is used a great deal in Lebanese cooking.

Aniseed
This is one of the oldest known spices. The seeds are oval and have a similar appearance to cumin and fennel. Ground aniseed is used in Lebanese biscuits and sweets. Aniseed oil is used in making the alcoholic beverage, arak.

Arak
Arak is an aniseed-based spirit distilled from grape juice. Now commercially available, arak used to be brewed in the villages of Lebanon.

Beans (*Loubyeh*)
Beans and pulses are commonly used in Lebanese recipes. Broad beans, butter beans, red kidney beans and green beans are most often used. Green beans are known as string beans.

Burghul
Cracked wheat. Burghul comes in various types: coarse, fine, white and wholemeal. It is the end product of wheat that has been boiled, dried in the sun and then sifted and crushed into fine or coarse particles. Burghul is one of the primary ingredients in kibbee, the national dish of Lebanon. It is readily available from Lebanese food stores, health food stores and supermarkets.

Cardamom (*Habit el hal*)
A member of the ginger family, best when crushed or ground at the time of use. One or two split cardamom pods are often added to coffee when it is brewed, giving a sweet aroma.

Carob molasses (*Dibis khoroub*)
Like aniseed, carob is known to have been used for centuries in the Middle East. The Lebanese use the carob bean to make a molasses, dibis khoroub.

Coriander seeds
These have a distinctive sweet, citrusy, peppery aroma and are best used when dry-roasted and then ground. They also have a medicinal, digestive property.

Cumin
A member of the parsley family, cumin is an essential spice in Lebanese cooking. It is readily available in kernels or already ground. Cumin seeds can be dry-roasted and crushed to release a strong, bittersweet aroma and taste.

Laban
Yoghurt.

Lamb
Lamb is almost always the meat used in Lebanese cookery. Lean backstraps are the choice cut, or you can use lamb leg. The meat must always be lean and freshly prepared.

Lebanese cucumbers
Essential in Lebanese food, Lebanese cucumbers are also known as pickling cucumbers. Their green skin is a shade lighter than that of the cucumber most commonly used in Australia, and they are not as long or as round as ridge or hot-house cucumbers. Do not substitute Australian cucumbers. You can use continental cucumbers.

Mahlab
Aromatic spice from the kernel of the black cherry, added to some desserts. It can produce a bitter taste if too much is used.

Marrow
Marrows are known as courgettes or Lebanese zucchini. Unlike zucchini the skin is a light-green colour. Marrows are also shorter and much rounder, and taste sweeter. I use 'baby marrow' – the small young ones are always tastier. Make sure the marrow is firm and the skin shiny.

M'jadra
Lentils or beans.

Okra
A green five-sided pod that has a distinctive gelatinous texture when cooked. The Lebanese always select small okra that are young and tender, and cook them whole. Okra can also be bought dried on a string or tinned.

Orange-blossom water
Liquid distilled from orange blossoms, used as a flavouring for desserts.

Pomegranate molasses (*Dibis roumman*)
Made by extracting the juice from pomegranate seeds and boiling it until it thickens and turns brown. It is used in soups and meat dishes to underscore a subtle, tangy flavour.

Purslane (*Baqli*)
A green, round-leafed member of the lettuce family, it is a distinctive ingredient in the Lebanese bread salad, fattoush (see page 44). It is also commonly eaten with vine leaves, tomatoes, olive oil, salt and pepper. Purslane is often difficult to obtain, so it is worth asking your greengrocer to let you know when it is in stock.

Rosewater
Distilled from fragrant rose petals and used as a flavouring for desserts, drinks and syrups.

Semolina
Widely used in Lebanese desserts, semolina is the flour obtained from milling either corn or the large, hard parts of wheat grain. The word also refers to the product obtained from the grinding of different cereal grains. I recommend using semolina made from wheat grain for these recipes.

Sterilised jars
To sterilise a glass jar, place the jar and the lid in a 120°C oven for 10 minutes. Turn off the heat, then leave the jar to cool in the oven. Take care to only handle the outside of the jar when removing and filling.

Sumac
A red-coloured spice made from the berries of the sumac bush. It has a distinctive, sharp, fruity taste similar to lemon. It is an essential ingredient in zah'tar and is often used in fish and chicken dishes as well as in salads.

Tahini
A thick, creamy paste made from ground sesame seeds. It is the basis of baba ghannooj and hummous dips, and is widely used in savoury dishes and sauces. Available at Middle Eastern stores and supermarkets.

Yoghurt culture (*Rowabe*)
Used in the making of yoghurt (laban). Whenever yoghurt is made, a small portion is taken from the fresh batch and used for making the next. It is common for family friends and community members to ask for a small amount of yoghurt culture from the person who makes a 'good batch'. If you do not have access to rowabe you can substitute good-quality, fresh natural yoghurt.

Zah'tar
A mixture of dried thyme, sumac and toasted sesame seeds. Zah'tar is Lebanese for 'thyme', but in recipes it is the dried mixture, not thyme alone, that is usually required. Zah'tar mixture is available at Middle Eastern food stores.

ACKNOWLEDGEMENTS

Again I've had the support of the 'usual suspects', especially my daughter Patricia and her wonderful friend, Raffaele Caputo. Many others were thanked in the first edition of this book, *The Lebanese Kitchen*, but there are a few new faces to whom I owe a debt of gratitude. First and foremost I must thank my dear friends Nada and Zahia for generously giving their time and assisting with testing the recipes. Invaluable also were Betty, Sarah, Fairouz and especially Janette, all of whom are from the kitchen at Abla's. And a very big thank you to my close friend, Kousirra, who shared her marvelous breadmaking skills with me. A nod of thanks to Maria Jevtic, Paul Martin and Suwan Jefferies for always being on call to taste-test each dish. And thank you to Judy Saba for her invaluable skills at checking the phonetic spelling of the recipe titles in Arabic.

To Ingrid Ohlsson, Kathleen Gandy, Megan Pigott, Evi Oetomo, Caroline Velik, Simon Griffiths (may you never snap another wedding photo again!), and Danie Pout, all of whom are perfectionists in everything they do. Thank you for 'turning out' such a wonderful cookbook. Finally, and again, I must thank Julie Gibbs for her enduring support and encouragement – you are a special person.

Index

LANTERN

Published by the Penguin Group
Penguin Group (Australia)
707 Collins Street, Melbourne, Victoria 3008, Australia
(a division of Penguin Australia Pty Ltd)
Penguin Group (USA) Inc.
375 Hudson Street, New York, New York 10014, USA
Penguin Group (Canada)
90 Eglinton Avenue East, Suite 700, Toronto, Ontario, Canada ON M4P 2Y3
(a division of Penguin Canada Books Inc.)
Penguin Books Ltd
80 Strand, London WC2R 0RL, England
Penguin Ireland
25 St Stephen's Green, Dublin 2, Ireland
(a division of Penguin Books Ltd)
Penguin Books India Pvt Ltd
11 Community Centre, Panchsheel Park, New Delhi – 110 017, India
Penguin Group (NZ)
67 Apollo Drive, Rosedale, North Shore 0632, New Zealand
(a division of Penguin New Zealand Pty Ltd)
Penguin Books (South Africa) (Pty) Ltd, Rosebank Office Park, Block D,
181 Jan Smuts Avenue, Parktown North, Johannesburg 2196, South Africa
Penguin (Beijing) Ltd
7F, Tower B, Jiaming Centre, 27 East Third Ring Road North,
Chaoyang District, Beijing 100020, China

Penguin Books Ltd, Registered Offices: 80 Strand, London WC2R 0RL, England

First published by Penguin Group (Australia), a division of Pearson Australia Group
Pty Ltd, 2010
This paperback edition was published by Penguin Group (Australia), 2012

3 5 7 9 10 8 6 4

Text copyright © Abla Amad 2010
Photography copyright © Simon Griffiths 2010

The moral right of the author has been asserted

Design by Danie Pout © Penguin Group (Australia)
Design coordination by Evi O.
Photography by Simon Griffiths
Styling by Caroline Velik
Typeset in FF Scala 11.5/13 pt by Post Pre-Press Group, Brisbane, Queensland
Colour reproduction by Splitting Image Colour Studio Pty Ltd, Clayton, Victoria
Printed and bound in China by Everbest Printing Co. Ltd.

National Library of Australia
Cataloguing-in-Publication data:

Amad, Abla, 1935 –
Abla's Lebanese Kitchen/by Abla Amad, photography by Simon Griffiths.
2nd ed.
ISBN 9781921383342 (pbk.)
Includes index.
Cookery, Lebanese.

641.595692

penguin.com.au/lantern